THE WORLD OF FOOD

Provincial France

The World of Food

❧

Provincial France

❧

by Monique Guillaume

WORLD PUBLISHING
TIMES MIRROR
NEW YORK

ACKNOWLEDGMENTS
British Consulting Editor: Katie Stewart, Cookery Editor of *The Times*
American Consulting Editor: Ann Seranne
Liaison Editor: Audrey Ellis
Photographs by Christian Délu (with the exception of those
on pp. 43, 52, 73, 75, 79, 117, 119, 123, 133, end papers)
Photographs by John Lee on pp. 52, 73, 79, 119

Published by The World Publishing Company
Published simultaneously in Canada
by Nelson, Foster & Scott Ltd.

First printing—1972

ISBN 0-529-04861-2
Library of Congress catalog card number: 72-85589
Printed in the United States of America
Designed by Terry McKee and Milton Charles

WORLD PUBLISHING
TIMES MIRROR

Contents

Glossary

à la: in the style or manner of; for example, *à la provençale* means in the style of Provence. Without a proper noun (*boeuf à la mode*), it means "in our style," or the style of the house. The American usage of à la mode—topped or accompanied by a scoop of ice cream—is unknown in France.

bain-marie: a large shallow pan of warm water in which a saucepan is placed to keep its contents warm. A bain-marie is also used to maintain slow even cooking on top of the stove and to prevent a crust from forming around such food as pâté, which cooks in the oven. A bain-marie differs from a double boiler in that the bottom of the top pan of the double boiler should never touch the simmering water in the pan beneath.

baste: to moisten with liquid, fat, or food juices during cooking to prevent drying and to add flavor.

beat: to thoroughly mix food or liquids by long and vigorous stirring with a spoon, fork, whisk, or electric beater. When beating egg whites make sure they are at room temperature when you start; they will mount more rapidly and to a greater volume than chilled whites. Correctly beaten egg whites will mount to 7 or 8 times their original volume. They will not mount stiffly at all if they contain even the tiniest particle of yolk or if the bowl or beater are moist or greasy. If your bowl is not an unlined copper one, beat a pinch of cream of tartar into the whites after you have beaten them for about 30 seconds. The cream of tartar acts as a stabilizer. If you use a whisk for beating, train yourself to use the muscles of your lower arm and wrist, as they tire less quickly than shoulder muscles. The whites are "stiffly beaten" when they will stand in stiff peaks on the wires of the beater.

paring knife   *slicing knife*   *chef's chopping knife*   *carving knife*   *sharpener*   *cleaver*

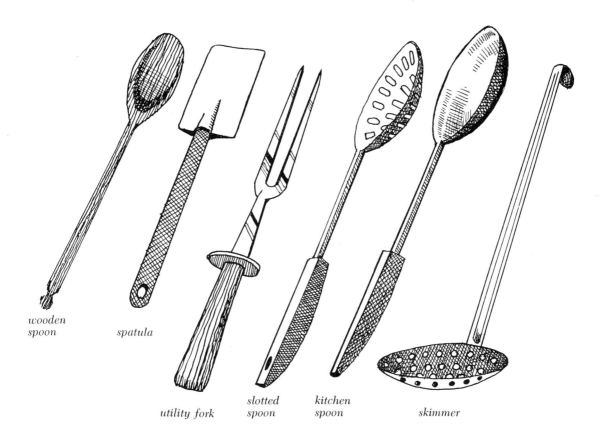

wooden spoon *spatula* *utility fork* *slotted spoon* *kitchen spoon* *skimmer*

beurre manié: a paste of uncooked butter and flour used as a thickening agent for sauces. Proportions are 3 tbs. flour and 2 tbs. softened butter. The two should be blended to a smooth paste with a fork before being incorporated into the sauce.

blanch: to plunge food into boiling water to soften, precook, partially cook, or to remove or reduce too strong a taste.

blend: to mix food or liquid in a manner less vigorous than beating.

bouquet garni: a combination of parsley, thyme, and bay leaf used for flavoring soups, stews, sauces, and vegetables. When a bouquet garni is called for place 2 or 3 parsley sprigs, a bay leaf, and ¼ tsp. dried thyme in a square of washed cheesecloth and tie it closed. A bundle is made so the herbs will not be skimmed off during cooking, and so they can be removed easily before serving.

braise: to brown, then simmer tightly covered, in a slow oven or over a low flame with a small amount of liquid.

butter: French butter is made from matured cream and is unsalted. When butter is specified in the recipes in this book, we mean first-grade butter made from sweet cream with no salt added. It is especially important to use unsalted butter when making pastry. When measuring butter, it is helpful to know that ¼-lb. stick equals 4 ounces, ½ cup, or 8 tbs.

cheese: the two cheeses most commonly used in French cooking are Swiss and parmesan. There are two types of imported Swiss cheese: true Gruyère, with small holes, and Emmenthal, which has a higher fat content and large holes. Domestic Swiss cheese can be substituted for imported and for that reason in these recipes we call merely for Swiss cheese. If you want to use the imported, and it will certainly add a note of authenticity to your dishes, buy the Gruyère.

chop: to cut food into small pieces. A large knife with a triangular blade is the best tool for chopping. Rest the blade of the knife on the food, holding the point down with your left hand. Hold the handle with your right hand and with rapid up-and-down movements, chop the food, swinging the knife in an arc to reach all the food on the chopping board. This technique is interchangeable with the one described for mincing.

colander: a bowl-shaped utensil, usually made of metal, which has perforations permitting its use as a strainer.

degrease: to remove accumulated fat from the surface of hot liquids. The easiest way is to place the liquid in the refrigerator, uncovered, until the fat sets. It will congeal on the surface and can easily be removed with a large spoon or skimmer. If the sauce, stock, or soup is simmering draw a large spoon over the surface. When the cooking is done, let the liquid settle for 5 minutes so the fat rises to the top. Then tip the pot and remove as much as you can with a spoon. It will take a few minutes. Whatever fat particles still remain can be blotted up with paper towels drawn over the surface. To remove fat from a pan in which meat is roasting, tilt the pan and collect the fat with a bulb baster. For stews and other casserole-cooked foods, again tip the pan and remove the fat with a large spoon. Alternatively, you can strain the sauce into another pan and degrease in the refrigerator as above.

dice: to cut food into small cubes, about ⅛ inch in size. To dice an onion or shallot, cut the vegetable in half horizontally, through the root. Lay the cut side down on the chopping board. With the knife pointing toward the root end, make several vertical cuts, leaving the slices attached to the root. Then make horizontal cuts through the onion or shallot from bottom to top, still leaving the slices attached to the root. Finally, slice downward to the board at ⅛-inch intervals and the onion or shallot will fall into dice.

double boiler: consists of two long-handled saucepans, one of which fits into the other. The food in the upper pan is cooked by the simmering water in the lower. A double boiler is used for cooking food that is quickly ruined by even a short period of overheating—egg yolks, chocolate, or cream, for example. Remember, the food in the upper pan should cook over, not in, hot water.

fatback: the strip of fat cut from the back of a hog carcass, usually cured by dry-salting.

foie gras: the liver of a goose or duck that has been fattened by forced feeding.

fold: to delicately blend a fragile mixture into a heavier mixture. When folding egg whites you must work gently but quickly so the whites lose as little of their volume as possible. After stirring 2 or 3 tbs. of the whites into the heavier mixture to lighten it, pour the remaining whites on top. With a spatula, cut down from the center of the mixture to the bottom of the pan, then quickly draw the spatula toward you against the edge of the pan. Continue with this motion while rotating the pan. With this technique, the heavier mixture at the bottom of the pan is brought up over the egg whites. It is better to have a few streaks of unblended white than to overfold and deflate the whites.

fry: to cook uncovered in hot fat. In deep-frying, the food is immersed in hot fat.

gratiné: to have a covering or crust which is achieved by browning the top of a sauced dish under the broiler. Bread crumbs and/or grated cheese and dots of butter help to create the light brown crust.

herbs: the aromatic leaves of annual or perennial plants. They thrive in temperate climates. Because fresh herbs are often unavailable in supermarkets you

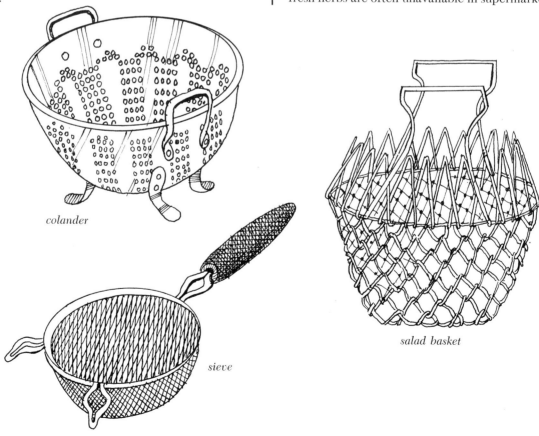

colander

sieve

salad basket

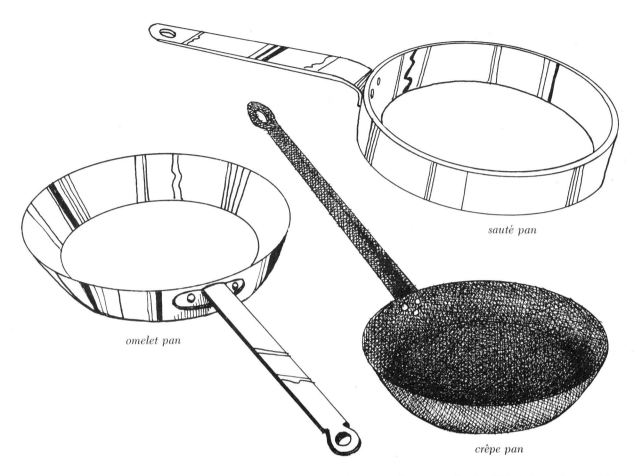

sauté pan

omelet pan

crêpe pan

ought to try your hand at growing your own: a small sunny plot or even a window box is all you need. Among the most frequently used herbs are parsley, basil, sage, thyme, tarragon, chervil, and bay leaves. When using herbs, don't use too much of any one kind or too many different kinds. If using dried herbs crush them between your fingertips or the palms of your hands before adding to the dish—this releases their flavor. Dried herbs quickly lose their strength and should be replenished at least once a year. They should be stored in tightly covered nonporous containers in the coolest, darkest spot in your kitchen.

knead: to work dough into a well-blended whole by repeatedly drawing it out and pressing it together with the knuckles and heel of the hand. The object in kneading is to make the dough perfectly smooth and to moisten and join all the gluten molecules. Although this end is invisible to the eye, the practiced hand will feel it because the dough becomes elastic.

marinade: a pickle or brine, or a mixture of wine or vinegar, oil, spices, and herbs.

marinate: to place food (generally meat) in a marinade for the purpose of absorbing or releasing flavor, or to tenderize it.

mince: to chop very finely. This is best done with a large, triangular-bladed knife. Grip the handle and top of the blade with your right hand, and hold the top of the pointed tip-end with your left hand. Chop with rapid, up-and-down movements, constantly brushing the ingredients into a heap in the center with the knife. This technique is interchangeable with the one described for chopping. Use the method you find more comfortable.

morels: delicately flavored mushrooms having a spongelike surface and elongated caps. In early spring morels are found growing wild in the United States. Canned or dried morels are imported from Europe and can be purchased in gourmet shops.

panbroil: to cook uncovered in a dry hot skillet.

poach: to submerge and cook food in a liquid that is barely simmering.

puree: to mash solid food into a fine pulp. This can be done in a food mill, a meat grinder, an electric blender, through a sieve, or in a mortar.

roast: to cook in an oven through dry heat or to cook on a spit over a fire.

reduce: to rapidly boil a liquid to reduce it in quantity and concentrate its flavor.

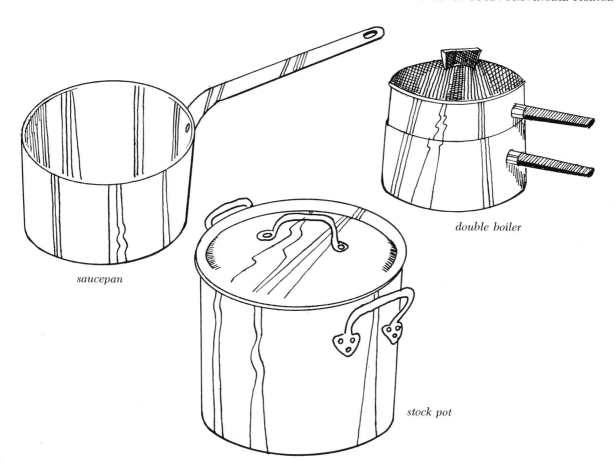

saucepan

double boiler

stock pot

roux: a mixture of butter and flour which is cooked slowly together and is used as a thickening agent for sauces. Proportions depend on the amount of sauce.

salt: its greatest culinary asset is to heighten the flavor of other foods. Before refrigeration, its powers of preservation were deemed its most important quality. Salt is rarely listed among the ingredients in the recipes in this book although it is almost always called for—it is so much a matter of taste that is has been left to the cook to "season to taste." When tasting for salt don't use only the tip of the tongue, but the middle and sides as well because that is where the greatest response to salt-stimulus lies. Unless otherwise specified table salt is called for. Coarse, or kosher, salt is occasionally listed. This is a square-grained sea salt containing natural iodine and other minerals. It is very flavorful and you might want to experiment with it as a substitute for table salt. It has more flavor than table salt, so use less. If you prefer to use it in a more finely grained state, mash the salt in a mortar. Coarse salt is sometimes called for in these recipes because it is effective in drawing moisture out of vegetables.

sauté: to cook and brown in a small amount of hot fat, usually in an open skillet on top of the stove. Food is sautéed as a preliminary step, to brown it, before fur-

ther cooking by another method; or it is sautéed until cooked through. For successful sautéeing, the fat should be very hot before the food is put into the pan. The food to be sautéed should be absolutely dry or it will not brown and sear properly; and the pan should not be crowded or the food will steam rather than brown.

scald: to heat to just below boiling, or around 190° F.

sift: to winnow, refine, or lighten (as flour or confectioners sugar) by passing through a sieve or sifter.

simmer: to cook food in liquid that is at a very low boil—the liquid should hardly move except for a bubble or two which barely breaks.

skim: to remove skin, fat, foam, or floating matter from the surface of a liquid, usually during cooking.

spices: the roots, barks, seeds, or fruit of aromatic perennial plants. They are normally grown in the tropics. Among the most frequently used spices is black pepper, which is processed from the green underripe fruit of an East Indian plant (*Piper nigrum*), and then cured. Pepper is not only remarkable as a preservative, but it strengthens food flavors without masking them. Pepper is always best freshly ground. One of the most important (and inexpensive) items of kitchen equipment you can buy is a pepper mill. White pepper is less pungent than black. It is made from the fully ripe berry from which the dark outer shell is removed. It is often used in light-colored sauces. Other important spices in cooking are cloves, ginger, allspice, nutmeg, and cinnamon. If you are using spices that are already ground, replenish them at least once a year because they rapidly lose their strength in this form. They should be stored in tightly covered nonporous containers in the coolest, darkest spot in your kitchen.

sugar: when sugar in called for in this book, the recipe requires granulated sugar—clear white crystals of purified raw sugar from which the molasses has been removed. *Superfine sugar* is a finer grind of granulated sugar. It dissolves rapidly and is used often for iced drinks. *Confectioners sugar*, also known as powdered sugar, is made by grinding and sifting granulated sugar. In order to lessen lumping, a small amount of cornstarch is added to it. It still usually contains lumps and should be sieved before using. In baking do not substitute it for granulated sugar. When confectioners sugar is required in these recipes it is specified.

stew: to cook slowly in a little liquid over a gentle flame, without boiling.

stock: the liquid obtained from the simmering together of meat, bones, vegetables, seasoning, and water. The flavor of good French food is usually the result of the stock used in its cooking, flavoring, or sauce. The French term for stock, *fonds de cuisine*, means literally, "foundation of cooking." This liquid, strained and reduced is the base for soups, the moistener for stews, braised meats, and vegetables, and the liquid used in making sauces that have a meat or fish flavoring. In making stock use what you have on hand (and it is a good idea to save meat scraps and beef, veal, and chicken bones in the freezer) plus fresh vegetables. Meat and bones give flavor and bones, in addition, give body to the stock. Do not use too many pork bones because pork tends to make the stock sweet. Lamb and ham bones are too strong in flavor for an all-purpose stock. Carrots, leeks, onions, and celery are the usual vegetables. Starchy vegetables will cloud the stock, and cauliflower, turnips, and the cabbage family are too strongly flavored. Remember never to let the liquid boil and never cover the kettle airtight or the stock will sour.

truss: to prepare a fowl for cooking by binding the wings and legs close to the body.

yeast: a living organism which is inactive when you buy it. It feeds on sugar and produces alcohol and carbon dioxide—the latter being the gas which makes dough rise. It can be bought in two forms: either as a fresh cake wrapped in silver paper or dry in a sealed envelope. Fresh cake yeast should be uniformly gray in color with no discoloration. It is perishable and will keep about a week under refrigeration. Dry-active yeast should be stored in a cool place and used before the expiration date stamped on the envelope.

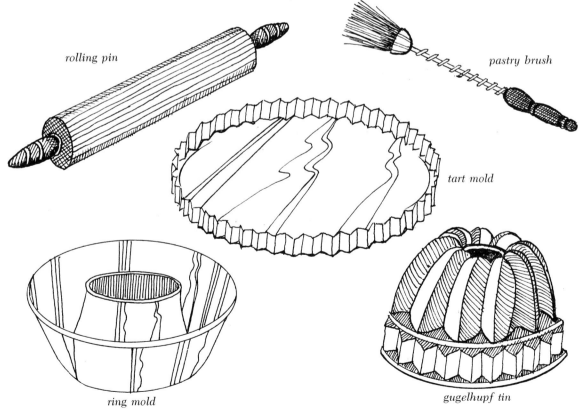

rolling pin

pastry brush

tart mold

ring mold

gugelhupf tin

Provincial France

The term "provincial cooking" can best be defined as regional food whose recipes are based upon indigenous ingredients. It is perhaps in France that provincial cooking reaches the highest levels—and with good reason, for all of France is a veritable garden of magnificent raw produce, each region having its own specialties.

While French provincial dishes are prepared with great care and skill, they are not subject to the elaborate, rich treatment associated with the famed haute cuisine. Provincial cooking avoids extravagance and pretension, and instead is based upon the concept that good cooking is achieved when the natural taste of the ingredients is brought out.

While nearly every part of France is famous for the creation of special dishes based on its local produce, ten somewhat distinct gastronomic regions based on historical rather than political divisions, can be discerned. An indication of the strength of French tradition is the fact that many of these special "regionalized" dishes have actually survived centuries without much, if any, change at all. On the pages that follow are some of the best of these time-honored recipes, along with a variety of others carefully chosen from a cross section of the most popular foods served in French homes and restaurants. Individually, they are a treat; together, they give you the flavor, authenticity, and attractiveness of the foods of all provincial France—a rare culinary delight.

Good food is an important part of French life, and mealtimes are enjoyed thoroughly. Yet, because the French housewife has traditionally been practical, sober, exceptionally discriminating in her marketing, and not given to extravagance in the preparation of her meals, the dishes she prepares are basically simple and economical. She makes a point of obtaining the best possible raw materials, and with these addresses herself to bringing out their full flavor. Her basic goal is to combine different ingredients to bring forth a delicious taste.

The eating habits of the French differ from ours. Generally, small breakfasts are eaten. Hot coffee with a roll and butter or a *croissant* (buttery crescent roll) is a popular breakfast.

Whereas our main meal of the day might consist of three or four courses, a French meal may well be composed of seven or eight courses served one after the other. Because of such eating habits, the French housewife's cooking is constantly on display. This undoubtedly contributes to the great pride and care that she brings to her art.

If the main meal of the day is at noontime, it might begin with pâté, followed by a sauté of chicken with herbs and tomatoes, vegetables, salad, cheese, fresh fruit, or perhaps a dessert such as a fruit tart, and, finally, coffee. A red or white table wine (*vin ordinaire*) and mineral water normally are drunk with the meal; the wine is finished with the cheese. An abundance of fresh bread is always on the table. Since the main meal is normally at midday, the evening meal is light.

The French are just as diet-conscious as we are. Indicative of this is a favorite saying of theirs: *"L'exces en tout est defaut"* ("Excess is always a fault"). Their tradition of eating only at mealtime also helps them to stay slim. Seldom will you find a Frenchman eating between meals. Obviously, French culinary habits are quite different from ours, so, with this book as your guide, prepare yourself for a first-class gastronomical trip to the world's capital of food—France.

In using this book, the reader will find it helpful to keep the following points in mind:
• Before preparing any dish, first read every step of the recipe and be sure you understand it. The recipe is your guide—always follow its directions step by step.
• Consider the amount of cooking time you have available when selecting recipes. Some meals take longer to prepare than others; and although the end result may justify the time required, your schedule for a particular day may well dictate which meal you can cook.
• Check your cooking equipment. Before embarking on a recipe read it thoroughly and be sure you have the proper utensils on hand and within easy reach. Do not try to make do with improper equipment.
• Naturally, you'll want to have *all* the ingredients called for. To make your cooking procedure as simple and enjoyable as possible, it is best to neatly lay out all the ingredients beforehand.

Normandy and the North

During the ninth century, the Vikings, or Northmen (from whom Normandy took its name), constantly ravaged this historical district of northwestern France. In 911 A.D. Charles the Simple, king of France, conceived of a solution to stop the destructive sieges: He gave Normandy to the Vikings, thereby making them responsible for it. After centuries of conquest and reconquest, the French finally regained Normandy in 1450.

The years of Scandinavian occupation and rule heavily influenced the customs, spirit, and physical appearance of the people who lived in this region, and these influences are still apparent today. Physically, the Normans closely resemble the Scandinavians. Many are tall, and have blue eyes and light hair. Rather solid and heavily built, the Normans are reputed to be bigger eaters than other Frenchmen.

The region is large. Its northern and western borders touch the English Channel, and there are many fashionable beach resorts, the most famous of which is Deauville.

Agriculturally, Normandy is a rich region. Norman sheep are considered to provide the best lamb in France. Norman cattle, raised for both beef and milk, also thrive on the excellent pasturage. The Norman cow, which probably is an ancestor of the Jersey, has an extremely high fat content in its milk, which results in excellent cream and butter. These dairy products are included in many of the characteristic dishes of the region. Chicken, vegetables, fish, veal, and soup typically are prepared with cream and butter by the Normans. Cheese is another of the dairy riches from the region, and important cheeses from Normandy include Camembert, Livarot, Pont l'Évêque, bondon of Neufchâtel, and Gervais cream cheese.

Fish is another specialty of Normandy. Coastal fishing along the English Channel yields a great variety of delicious fish, including sole, turbot, whiting, conger eel, and skate. Shellfish are also abundant: Lobster, oysters, shrimp, prawns, crayfish, clams, crabs, and sea urchins are widely available. Plump, succulent mussels from the natural mussel beds are so reasonable in price that everyone can afford them. They are cooked in many different ways—in cream, cider, Calvados, white wine, butter, and frequently in soup. Freshwater fish are also plentiful.

Normandy is the principal apple-growing area of France, and apples are an important ingredient in Norman cooking. In addition to their use in preserves and jellies, apples are used to prepare many of the regional meat and poultry specialties, such as *poulet Vallée d'Auge.*

Because there are no vineyards in Normandy, no wine is produced there. Apple cider is often drunk throughout the meal. Calvados, the distilled juice of the apple, is used in the preparation of many sauces, much in the manner that cooks from other regions use wine. An ancient Norman custom still practiced today is the *trou normand,* or "Norman hole" —a glass of Calvados drunk at intervals during the meal to help digest the food and revive the appetite so that one can continue eating. The "hole" refers to the pause in the eating (or perhaps to the alcohol-created hole in the stomach).

Benedictine, the liqueur distilled from herbs that grow on the seaside cliffs of Normandy, is made in the Fécamp area, where it was first produced by the monk Dom Bernardo Vincelli in 1510. It is a combination of 30 herbs with brandy, honey, and sugar and was first used as a restorative for the weary monks at the abbey at Fécamp, whose strict schedules allowed for only a few hours sleep each night. Benedictine was also used in the treatment of malarialike diseases that were quite common then. The initials D.O.M. that appear on every bottle of Benedictine stand for *Deo Optimo Maximo*—"To God most good, most great."

Although most rich meals end with cheese and fruit, Norman cooks are highly proficient in the fine art of dessert making. Their recipes were created, as all other regional dishes were, to utilize the most abundant products of the area. Apples, poached, baked, and in pies and tarts are a natural choice for desserts of the region. And the Normans also have a special way with baked goods. The abundance of rich cream and butter is an added incentive to any good cook and the Norman bakers produce fine cakes and breads.

Normandy's particularly good agricultural produce, its fine pasturage for the raising of cattle and sheep, its production of rich butter, cream, and cheese, and the availability and variety of fish, fruits, game, and poultry, have combined to create one of the most highly developed cuisines in France.

Sole and Mussels

SOLES À LA CRÈME

Serves 4

1¾ cups dry white wine
2 shallots, peeled and chopped
8 parsley sprigs
1½ qts. mussels, trimmed, scrubbed, and cleaned
2 lbs. fillet of sole
1 cup heavy cream
1 tsp. cornstarch
juice of 1 lemon
⅓ cup grated Swiss cheese
2 tbs. bread crumbs
2 tbs. butter

Mussels need long and careful cleaning to remove sand, slime, and grit. Scrub each one with a rough brush under cold running water. With a small knife or scissors remove the beard. Set them in a basin of water for an hour or two. Remove to a colander, drain, and wash again. They are ready to be cooked.

There is no genuine sole in American waters. Fish sold here as sole is generally flounder, which is perfectly suitable for this recipe.

Combine the wine, shallots, and parsley in a large shallow saucepan and bring to a boil. Add the mussels, cover, and cook quickly until they open—about 5 minutes. Remove the pan from the heat and lift out the mussels. Remove and discard any mussels that remain closed. Discard the shells but reserve the wine in which the mussels were cooked. Let it cool.

Preheat the oven to 400.

Pour the wine into the pan and add the fish fillets. Cover and bring just to a boil. Carefully remove the fillets with a spatula and place them in a shallow, greased baking dish. Add the mussels.

Mix together the cream, cornstarch, lemon juice, and half the cooking liquid from the fish. Bring to a boil and stir constantly until the sauce thickens. Taste for seasoning. Pour the sauce over the fillets and the mussels, sprinkle with the grated cheese and bread crumbs, and dot with butter. Place in the preheated oven and heat through for about 5 minutes. Then broil quickly to brown.

Creamed Brussels Sprouts

CHOUX DE BRUXELLES À LA CRÈME

Serves 4

2 lbs. Brussels sprouts
¼ cup butter
juice of 1 lemon
1¼ cups heavy cream

This unusual way of preparing Brussels sprouts is an excellent accompaniment to roasts.

Trim and discard the outer loose leaves and base of the stalks of the sprouts. Make two shallow cuts across the base of each sprout and wash quickly in cold water. Cook them for 15 minutes in a large uncovered saucepan of rapidly boiling water. Drain and sprinkle lightly with pepper.

Melt the butter in a skillet, add the sprouts, and saute over moderate heat for a few moments, shaking the pan frequently. Puree the sprouts in a food mill and return them to the same pan. Sprinkle with the lemon juice and cook for a few minutes over very low heat, gradually adding the cream with a spoon. Do not allow to boil. Serve in a heated vegetable dish.

Baked Herring Fillets

HARENGS AU VIN ROUGE

Serves 4

4 large potatoes, peeled
2 tbs. butter
1 large onion, peeled and sliced into rings (about 1 cup)
3 tbs. minced parsley
1 shallot, peeled and stuck with 2 cloves
8 fresh herring fillets
2 bay leaves, crumbled
2 dried juniper berries, crushed
¾ cup red wine
1 tsp. sugar
3 peppercorns

This dish is especially popular in Boulogne. It makes an excellent first course or even a main course for a light evening meal.

Preheat the oven to 400.

Cook the potatoes in boiling water for 10 minutes; drain, slice thinly, and dry them. Grease a large baking dish with the butter. Arrange the potato slices, onion rings, parsley, and shallot over the bottom of the dish. Place the herring fillets on top and sprinkle on the bay leaves and juniper berries. Add the wine and, finally, the sugar, peppercorns, and a pinch of salt. Bake for 25 minutes. Remove the shallot and serve the fish in the baking dish.

To be really good, Calvados requires a long aging period. Unfortunately, truly aged Calvados is rare in the United States. If you have some, certainly use it. But rather than use an immature Calvados, substitute a good American applejack.

Chicken with Apples and Cream

POULET VALLÉE D'AUGE

Serves 4

1 2-lb. frying chicken
4 tbs. butter
2 shallots, peeled and chopped
2 tbs. minced parsley
2 tbs. fresh chopped, or 1 tsp. dried chervil
¾ cup dry white wine or cider
pinch of sugar
6 medium baking apples, peeled, cored, and quartered
¾ cup water
pinch of cinnamon
⅓ cup Calvados or applejack
1 cup heavy cream

This pleasing way of preparing a chicken is typically Norman—combining apples, cream, chicken, and Calvados to make a delicious dish.

Dry the chicken. Melt the butter in a sauté pan with a tight-fitting lid. Add the shallots, parsley, and chervil. Add the chicken and brown on all sides. Gradually add the wine or cider. Season with salt and pepper and add the sugar. Cover and cook over low heat for about 1 hour.

While the chicken is cooking, place the apples in a saucepan with the water and cinnamon; cover and cook until the apples are just tender, but not mushy. Lift the cooked chicken out of the pan, cut it into serving portions, and place on a heated platter. Add the apples, Calvados or applejack, and the cream to the liquid in which the chicken was cooked. Heat together for a moment but do not boil. Pour the sauce over the chicken and serve.

This dish is a specialty of the coast of Normandy, where lobsters are plentiful. Where available, crayfish can be substituted for lobster.

Preheat the oven to 400.

Plunge the live lobster head first into a large pot of rapidly boiling salted water. Cook for five minutes and drain. Dot the fleshy underside of the lobster with small pieces of butter and season with salt and pepper. Butter a large sheet of foil, place the lobster in the center, and wrap it completely. Set on a large baking dish or tray and bake for 45 minutes. If you buy a precooked lobster, bake for only 20 minutes.

While the lobster is baking, prepare the sauce. In a saucepan mix the cream with the mustard, capers, cornstarch, salt, and pepper. Heat the mixture over moderate heat, stirring constantly, until it just reaches the boiling point. Remove from heat.

Cut the hot lobster in half and serve with boiled rice. Offer the sauce separately or pour it over the lobster.

Lobster with Mustard Sauce

HOMARD EN CHEMISE

Serves 2

1 live lobster, about 2 lbs.
3 tbs. butter

FOR THE SAUCE:
1½ cups heavy cream
3 tbs. prepared mustard
1 tb. capers, drained
1 tb. cornstarch

This is a traditional Belgian recipe much appreciated in France. The beer gives the beef a distinctive and delicate flavor; it should be served with this dish.

Dry the cubes of beef and season with salt and pepper. Melt the lard in a large skillet and sauté the diced bacon, along with one of the chopped onions. Add the beef and brown evenly over high heat. Add the remaining onions and cook for a few minutes, still over high heat. Sprinkle with flour and stir for 2 or 3 minutes. Gradually add the beer, then the juniper berries, and sugar. Cover and cook over low heat for 1½ hours. Just before serving, stir in the vinegar.

Beef Braised in Beer

CARBONNADE À LA FLAMANDE

Serves 4

2 lbs. lean beef from the chuck, rump, or round, cubed
¼ cup lard
¼ lb. fat bacon, diced
6 large onions, peeled and chopped (about 5 cups)
3 tbs. all-purpose flour
2 cups beer or ale
4 dried juniper berries, crushed
1 tsp. sugar
¼ cup vinegar

French puff pastry is many leaves of dough separated by many leaves of butter. A half-inch piece will puff to 4 or 5 inches in the oven and is magnificently light and flaky to bite into. It is not difficult to make but it is a time-consuming procedure because of the many resting periods required. The dough should always be cold and if possible you should work on a cool, smooth marble surface. Closely covered puff-pastry dough will keep in the refrigerator for several days; wrapped airtight, it freezes perfectly for many months.

Partridge Pie

TOURTE DE PERDREAUX

Serves 4 to 6

FOR THE PUFF PASTRY:
4 cups sifted all-purpose flour
1½ cups ice water
1½ cups plus 4 tbs. chilled butter
1 egg, beaten, for glazing

FOR THE FILLING:
2 partridges, plucked, singed, and
    cleaned
2 tbs. butter
1 lb. veal, ground
2 tbs. minced parsley
2 tbs. minced chervil
1 tb. fresh chopped, or ½ tsp. dried
    thyme
pinch of mixed spices
2 eggs, beaten
⅓ cup dry white wine
1 small can truffles
    (optional)
8 slices bacon, finely diced
5 tbs. Calvados, applejack, or
    Cognac

This recipe is suitable for almost any game bird: pheasants or pigeons, for example. The size of the birds must be considered: one large pheasant would suffice where two pigeons would be required.

To make the puff pastry, sift the flour in a heap on a floured board and make a well in the center. Into this well pour the ice water and a pinch of salt. Knead lightly with your fingertips and form the pastry into a ball. Let it rest, covered, for 30 minutes in the refrigerator.

After 30 minutes, roll the pastry into a large circle. Scatter small pieces of butter in the middle of this circle and fold the pastry to enclose the butter, as if making a parcel. Sprinkle with flour and roll out very lightly into a long narrow rectangle. The pieces of butter will stick out. Bring the bottom third up and the top third down, as if folding a long letter. Turn it a quarter of the way around. Roll out again into a long, narrow rectangle, sprinkle with flour, and again fold it 3 times. Let it rest in the refrigerator for 20 minutes. Repeat the process; that is, roll the pastry into a long, narrow rectangle, fold it 3 times, and repeat twice, turning the pastry a quarter of the way around each time after folding. Let it rest again for 20 minutes. Begin the process again. In France, this is called giving 6 turns to the pastry. Proceed with the recipe while the pastry is resting.

Preheat the oven to 400.

Discard the partridge heads but save the livers for another use. Rub the birds with butter. Roast them in the preheated oven or on a spit for 25 minutes, basting occasionally with the pan juices. Then joint, bone, and skin the birds. Mix the ground veal with the parsley, chervil, thyme, spices, beaten eggs, wine, optional truffles, and a seasoning of salt and pepper.

On a floured board thinly roll out the puff pastry. Divide it into 2 parts, one larger than the other. Line the bottom of a buttered 9-inch tart mold or pie plate with the larger piece. Remove the bacon rind and put half the bacon on the pastry. Cover with half the prepared filling. Put pieces of boned partridge on top. Cover with the remaining filling, and then the remaining bacon. Finally, put on the pastry lid, pressing the edges together with your fingertips. Make a small round hole in the center for the steam to escape during cooking. Pour the Calvados through this opening. Brush with the beaten egg. Cook in the preheated oven for 1 hour. The pie can be served hot or cold.

The black truffle is a round and wrinkled mushroom which grows underground. It has a pungent scent and a slightly licorice flavor. Pigs and dogs are trained to sniff truffles out of the ground and then must be cajoled into relinquishing possession. Black truffles are usually added to dishes and sauces for the sake of their aroma.

Tripe Casserole

TRIPES À LA MODE DE CAEN

Serves 6

3 small carrots, thinly sliced
4 leeks, cleaned and thinly sliced
3 large onions, peeled and thinly
    sliced (about 3 cups)
3 lbs. tripe
1 large onion, peeled and stuck
    with 3 cloves
1 tsp. dried thyme
2 bay leaves
1 calf's foot or foreshank
1 cup Calvados or applejack
4½ cups cider or dry white wine

> To prepare leeks for cooking,
> remove the coarse outer leaves,
> cut off the root end, and make
> vertical cuts through the leaves
> from the top of the white part.
> Hold under cold running water
> to loosen the grit and mud.
> Place each head down in cold
> water for a few minutes. Before
> cooking examine again for dirt.

This dish, popular throughout France, originated in the Norman city of Caen. To save yourself the necessary preliminaries of scraping, washing, and blanching, buy tripe that is ready to cook.

Preheat the oven to 250.

Line a large earthenware casserole with the sliced vegetables. Place the tripe, cut into thin strips, on top. Add the herbs, the whole onion, the calf's foot, salt and pepper to taste, the Calvados or applejack, and enough cider to just cover. Put on the lid and encase it with a dampened floured cloth to minimize evaporation. Cook for 10 hours, regulating oven temperature so that the tripe cooks at a slow simmer. When done, tripe should be tender but still retain its texture. Remove surface fat, discard the calf's foot and the onion stuck with cloves, and serve directly from the casserole.

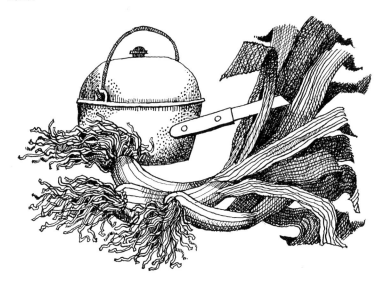

Serve these little cookies as snacks or to accompany a fruit dessert. They are a specialty of Trouville.

Preheat the oven to 400.

Measure the sifted flour into a mixing bowl and add the butter, cut into small pieces. Using your fingertips, rub the butter into the flour. Add the sugar and a pinch of salt, then the egg yolks and the vanilla. Mix thoroughly. Shape the dough into a ball and let rest in a cool place, covered with a cloth. Roll the dough out to a thickness of ¼ inch on a floured board. Cut into whatever shapes you like and place the shapes of dough on a baking sheet. Bake in the preheated oven for about 10 minutes, or until the cookies are golden brown.

Sweet Butter Cookies

BISCUITS SABLÉS

Makes 5 to 6 dozen

3 cups sifted all-purpose flour
1 cup butter
½ cup sugar
2 egg yolks
few drops vanilla extract

Brittany

Brittany's culture can be traced most directly to the Celts of Britain, who were forced out of the British Isles in the fifth century and settled on the Armoricain peninsula, which they named Brittany. The Celts also contributed the Breton language to the region, which today is still spoken by over a million people. It was not until the sixteenth century, after a succession of royal marriages, that Brittany became part of France.

The hearty and rugged nature of the land is reflected in the cuisine of Brittany, simple and without artiface. The top-quality ingredients receive no elaborate preparation.

Brittany is dominated by the sea. Its waters abound in many varieties of fish, and one of its major industries is deep-sea fishing. In addition to the renowned lobsters and several types of succulent oysters, clams, mussels, periwinkles, cockles, scallops, crabs, crayfish, sole, mackerel, mullet, sardines, and bass are taken from Breton waters and distributed throughout France.

The unique flavor of the highly esteemed lamb and mutton of Brittany is also attributable to the sea. This subtle, slightly salty meat comes from sheep that graze on the aromatic grasses of the brackish salt-meadow pastures (*prés-salés*) along the seashore. *Gigot de prés-salés* (leg of lamb from a sheep fed on the *prés-salés*) is a prized dish in restaurants and homes throughout France.

Even inland the presence of the unseen ocean is felt: fine cabbage, artichokes, carrots, and potatoes are grown on farmlands fertilized with seaweed. The fruit, too, is excellent, especially the apples, and strawberries from Plougastel.

A culinary specialty of Brittany unrelated to the sea is the *crêpe*, or pancake. Made from either buckwheat flour or wheat flour, it is served as appetizer, entrée, or dessert, depending upon the batter and the filling. A typical appetizer or entrée *crêpe* would be made with buckwheat flour and filled with ham, crabmeat, chicken, or cheese; a dessert *crêpe* could be made with wheat flour and filled with jam or honey. A food of great adaptability, *crêpes* are offered everywhere in Brittany.

Suckling pig is another specialty of Brittany. In Redon it is stuffed and cooked whole on the spit. Parisians consider Breton suckling pig a delicacy, and often serve it in aspic. Around Auray, pork is made into *andouillettes* (small herb-flavored tripe sausages), which are delicious broiled and served with apple puree. Morlaix is famous for its smoked cured ham. Breton partridge and hare have an especially pungent flavor, and the fowl of this region, particularly that from around Rennes, the capital, is of the first quality. As with their seafood, the Bretons rely on the natural flavor of the raw ingredients and avoid elaborate modifications of their taste.

Rich and sophisticated sauces are hardly used at all in Brittany except in the Loire Valley. It is there that one would find the delicious *beurre blanc* served. A reduction of shallots, wine, and vinegar to which butter is added, this sauce was conceived to counteract the dryness of freshwater fish. It has become so popular, that any excuse to eat it is used.

Brittany is not a wine-growing area. Its most famous wine is muscadet, a dry fruity wine produced around Nantes, at the extreme southern boundary of Brittany. Like the Norman, the Breton generally prefers to drink cider made from locally grown apples. These apples are also distilled into a brandy similar to Calvados.

With an abundance of fine-quality raw materials, Breton cooks produce some of the simplest and heartiest French provincial dishes. There are restaurants in the region where you will be served excellent flamed crab and sophisticated *homard à l'américaine,* but throughout the greater part of Brittany you will be served fresh local products, simply cooked and honestly presented.

Breakfast in Brittany is traditionally a simple affair: Toasted bread spread with butter and served with a pot of hot coffee and milk. Before those breakfast dishes have disappeared, the solemn preparation of the midday and evening meals has usually begun.

A Breton midday meal will normally include one seafood dish accompanied by an assortment of vegetables and a selection of local cheese, and of course, a glass of cider for the digestion.

The nights in Brittany are often damp and chilly and a hearty meal served before a crackling fire helps to drive away the cold. A substantial soup, followed by meat or poultry, vegetables, and then fresh fruit or perhaps *crêpes* for dessert. If it is to be *crêpes*, then hard cider must be served for all Bretons know that it is the only acceptable drink to accompany them.

Flamed Crab

CRABE FLAMBÉ

Serves 6

1 2½–3 lb. crab
½ cup dry white wine
½ cup dark rum or scotch
2 tbs. minced parsley
1 cup tomato juice

Live, precooked, or canned crab may be used in this recipe. It can be served with rice if you wish to make it a substantial main dish, or just as it is for a first course.

If you buy a live crab, plunge it into a deep kettle of boiling water for 5 minutes. Then place the crab in a large pot with ½ cup of dry white wine. Cover and steam for 10 to 15 minutes. Cool the crab before removing the flesh from the shell.

Warm the crab meat and the rum or scotch in a skillet over low heat. Remove the skillet from the heat and, averting your face, ignite the rum with a match. Shake the skillet gently so that the flames spread all over the crab. When the flames die out, add salt and pepper, the minced parsley, and the tomato juice. Bring to a boil, stir the sauce, and serve immediately.

ও

Flamed Sautéed Chicken

POULET SAUTÉ À LA
MODE DE TRÉGUIER

Serves 4

¼ cup butter
1 tb. oil
2 tbs. minced parsley
2 shallots, peeled and chopped
1 3-lb. frying chicken, cut into
    pieces
¾ cup dry white wine
⅓ cup Cognac
¼ lb. small mushrooms, wiped
    clean
5 slices bacon, diced
¾ cup tomato juice
few sprigs fresh chervil and
    tarragon, chopped

A tasty way of cooking a young chicken. The Cognac, herbs, and wine give delicious flavor to the sauce.

Heat the butter and oil together in a large, heavy skillet. Add the parsley and the shallots, and sauté them gently until they are golden. Add the chicken pieces and sauté over high heat, turning until they are golden on all sides. Add the white wine, a tablespoon at a time, to prevent the chicken from sticking; lower the heat, and cover. After about 30 minutes, when the chicken is tender, remove the skillet from the heat. Add the (warmed) Cognac and, averting your face, ignite the Cognac with a match. Shake the skillet until the flames die. Return to the heat, cover, and continue cooking gently for a few minutes. Add the mushrooms, bacon, and tomato juice. Cook over high heat until the liquid is reduced. Taste for seasoning. Transfer to a heated serving dish, sprinkle with the chopped chervil and tarragon, and serve.

Fried Mussels

MOULES FRITES

Serves 4

2 qts. mussels
¼ cup dry white wine
sprig of fresh, or ½ teaspoon dried
    thyme
2 eggs
¼ cup toasted bread crumbs
1 cup heavy cream
juice of ½ lemon
2 tbs. minced parsley
1 tb. cornstarch
1 cup peanut oil

This is an unusual first course which is very popular in Brittany. The crisply fried mussels contrast well with the creamy sauce.

Scrub the mussels well under running water, brushing them to remove seaweed, sand, and grit. Remove the beards. Place the wine and the thyme in a large saucepan and bring to a boil. Add the mussels, cover, and cook very quickly until they open. Lift the mussels from the pan with a slotted spoon, discarding any that have not opened, and cool in a strainer. Reserve the cooking liquid. When the mussels are cool, remove them from the shells.

Beat the eggs in a large bowl and season with salt and pepper. Spread the bread crumbs on a plate. Dip the mussels in the beaten egg and then roll them in the bread crumbs, coating them well. Set aside while preparing the sauce.

Mix the cream, lemon juice, half the strained liquid in which the mussels were cooked, parsley, and cornstarch together in a saucepan. In a large skillet heat the oil until it is hot, but not smoking. Add the mussels and fry over high heat, turning until they are golden. Drain on paper towels. Bring the ingredients for the sauce to a boil, stirring constantly. Pour the sauce into a warmed sauce boat and serve with the mussels.

Mussels Gratiné

MOULES À LA
LORIENTAISE

Serves 10

3½ qts. mussels
1 cup dry white wine
1 shallot, peeled
few sprigs parsley
3 bay leaves
4 cups white bread crumbs, lightly
    packed
¼ cup butter

In this region, mussels are widely used. This is a very simple and delicious first course that is quick to prepare.

Scrub the mussels well under running water, brushing them to remove seaweed, sand, and grit. Remove the beards. Put the white wine into a large saucepan with salt and pepper to taste, the shallot, parsley, and bay leaves. Bring the liquid to a boil and add the mussels. Cover and cook for about 5 minutes over high heat. When the mussels have opened, take them out of the pan with a slotted spoon, discarding any that haven't opened, and remove half the shell of each one. Place the mussels in an ovenproof dish, each one lying in its remaining half shell. Sprinkle with the bread crumbs. Place a small piece of butter on each, and moisten with the strained liquid in which they were cooked. Broil quickly. Serve immediately.

The origin of this name is endlessly disputed. All agree, however, that the dish is a splendid creation.

To kill the lobster, cut ½ inch down into its back at the point where chest and tail join; this will kill the lobster instantly. Then plunge it head first into a kettle of boiling water. Divide the tail into 4 pieces, and split each claw into 2 pieces. Remove the pocket near the head.

Preheat the oven to 350.

Heat the oil in a heavy skillet or casserole and add all the lobster pieces except the head. Season with salt and pepper and cook over high heat until the lobster pieces turn red. Pour off some of the hot fat. Sprinkle with Cognac and white wine. Lower the flame and heat for a second. Remove the casserole from the stove; turning your face, ignite the Cognac with a match and shake the skillet until the flames die. Place the casserole over the heat once again and add the shallots, garlic, beef stock, fish stock, cayenne pepper, and tomatoes. Cover and cook in preheated oven for 15 to 20 minutes.

While the lobster is cooking, blend the chervil and tarragon with the butter. Remove the lobster from the oven. Take out the pieces and remove all the meat from the shell (or you can serve the meat in the shell). Place on a heated serving plate. Strain the sauce and add the herb butter to it in small pieces, stirring until the butter is melted and the sauce well bound together. Pour the sauce over the lobster and sprinkle with lemon juice. Serve immediately.

Lobster with Wine and Herbs

HOMARD À L'AMÉRICAINE

Serves 3 to 4

1 live lobster, about 2 lbs.
6 tbs. oil
3 tbs. Cognac
¼ cup dry white wine
2 shallots, peeled and chopped
1 clove garlic, crushed
1 tb. beef stock
⅔ cup fish stock
large pinch cayenne pepper
3 tomatoes, peeled, seeded, and juiced
few sprigs fresh chervil and tarragon, finely chopped, or ¼ tsp. each dried
¼ cup plus 2 tbs. butter
juice of 1 lemon

To make fish stock combine the following in a large saucepan: 2 lbs. fish bones, heads, tails, skins, and trimmings, 1 thinly sliced onion, 1 tsp. lemon juice, ½ tsp. salt, 1 cup dry white wine, and water to cover. Simmer uncovered for 30 minutes, strain, and correct seasoning. A good emergency substitute is 1½ cups bottled clam juice combined with 1 cup each white wine and water, the onion, and lemon juice. Do not add salt. Simmer for 30 minutes, reducing the liquid to 2 cups. If it is too salty, dilute with water.

Scallops in White Wine

COQUILLES ST. JACQUES AU MUSCADET

Serves 6

2 tbs. butter
2 shallots, peeled and chopped
2 tbs. minced parsley
16 sea scallops, each sliced into 2
    or 3 pieces
¼ cup dry white wine, preferably
    muscadet or Chablis

Coquilles St. Jacques makes a pleasant and easily prepared first course. It is usually served in attractive scallop shells of about 1/3-cup capacity.

Melt the butter in a skillet and sauté the shallots and parsley for a few moments. Add the scallops and cook over high heat for 5 minutes, turning the pieces until they are golden. Season with salt and quite a lot of pepper. Remove the skillet from the heat and spoon the scallops into individual shells or a warm serving dish. Pour the wine into the skillet and bring quickly to a boil. Pour over the scallops and serve.

TO DICE AN ONION OR SHALLOT

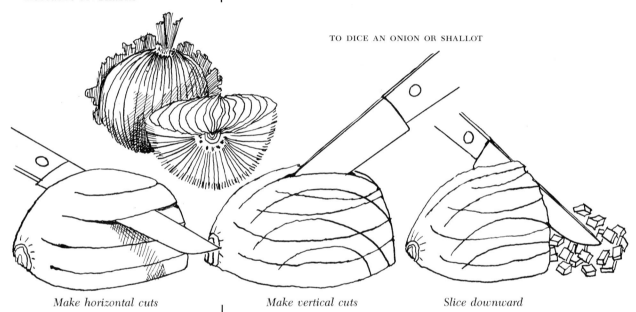

Make horizontal cuts   *Make vertical cuts*   *Slice downward*

Roast Pork with Cider

PORC AU CIDRE

Serves 4

1½ lbs. pork tenderloin
few leaves fresh chopped, or
    1 tsp. dried sage
8 baking apples, cored but whole
2 tbs. butter
¼ tsp. nutmeg
1 cup cider or dry white wine

This is a very pleasing dish, especially in winter. The sharp taste is most appetizing.

Preheat the oven to 425.

Place the pork in an ovenproof baking dish. Sprinkle the meat with the sage, salt, and pepper. Roast for 50 minutes, turning the meat occasionally to brown on all sides.

Spread the top of the apples with butter and sprinkle with nutmeg. Heat the cider. Lower the oven to 350. Pour the warmed cider over the pork and surround it with the prepared apples. Roast for an additional 30 minutes. Serve in the baking dish.

When strawberries are in season, this is an economical dessert, suitable for family meals and entertaining. The crust must be baked before adding the filling. Be sure to remove the butter from the refrigerator 1 hour before you begin.

Preheat the oven to 400.

Sift the flour into a bowl and make a well in the center. Add the egg yolks, softened butter, salt, water, and sugar. Mix very quickly, rubbing between your fingertips until a shortcake dough is obtained. Form the dough into a ball. Let it rest in a cool place for 20 minutes. After the 20 minutes, roll out the dough on a floured board. Line a 9-inch greased tart mold or pie plate with the dough. To prevent the center from rising, prick with a fork, line carefully with foil or wax paper, and fill with dried beans. Bake for 25 minutes in the preheated oven. Cool for 10 minutes before removing beans and foil.

While the crust is baking, prepare the confectioners custard. Mix the confectioners sugar and the egg yolks together in a saucepan. Add the flour and mix thoroughly. Stirring constantly, gradually add the milk. Then add the vanilla bean or vanilla extract, and a pinch of salt. Place the pan over low heat and bring to a boil, stirring constantly with a wooden spoon until the mixture has thickened. Remove from the heat. Lift out the vanilla bean (if used) and add the butter, stirring vigorously. Let the mixture cool until it is lukewarm.

Pour the custard gently into the cooked pastry, smoothing with a spatula. Quickly wash the strawberries and pat dry with paper towels. Place them carefully on top of the custard. Melt the jelly in a small pan over low heat. Spoon it over the strawberries. Let cool before serving.

Strawberry Custard Pie

TARTE AUX FRAISES

Serves 6 to 8

FOR THE PASTRY:
1¾ cups sifted all-purpose flour
2 egg yolks
¼ cup butter, softened
¼ tsp. salt
3 tbs. water
¼ cup sifted confectioners sugar

FOR THE CONFECTIONERS CUSTARD:
1 cup sifted confectioners sugar
2 egg yolks
½ cup sifted all-purpose flour
1 cup milk
½ vanilla bean or few drops vanilla
  extract
2 tbs. butter

FOR THE FILLING:
1 quart of strawberries
½ cup red currant or raspberry
  jelly

You needn't throw away the unused egg whites. They freeze quite well in a plastic bag or freezer container. Thaw them in the refrigerator before using. Before beating, the whites should be brought to room temperature. One egg white equals about 1½ tbs.

Breton Pancakes

LES CRÊPES

Serves 8

4 eggs
⅓ cup dark rum
2 tbs. oil
¾ cup beer
1¾ cups buckwheat flour
1 cup water
lard or bacon fat
sugar

The Bretons eat pancakes as the rest of the French eat bread.

Beat the eggs in a large bowl along with the rum, oil, and a pinch of salt. Gradually add the beer and the flour, stirring constantly with a wooden spoon until the mixture is smooth. Cover with a cloth and let stand in a warm place for at least an hour. Then add the water.

Heat a small skillet (ideally, one kept exclusively for crêpes) and rub with a piece of lard or bacon fat. Pour 3 or 4 tablespoons of the batter into the pan and tip it so that the batter spreads all over the bottom of the pan. As soon as the crêpe is covered with little golden holes, turn it over. Cook a moment longer; then slide onto a plate.

In Brittany, the first pancake is given to the birds for luck; you should use yours to test the consistency of your batter and the amount of batter needed for each crêpe.

Grease the skillet again, and cook a second crêpe in the same way. Pile them on top of each other on a heated dish, dusting each lightly with sugar. Serve the crêpes with melted butter, honey, or jam.

Strawberry Jam

CONFITURE DE FRAISES

Makes about 4 pints

1½ qts. strawberries
5 cups sugar
⅔ cup water

The strawberries of Brittany are famous throughout France. There are several methods of making strawberry jam, but this is one of the author's favorites.

Hull the strawberries and wash them quickly and carefully. Mix the sugar and the water in a large saucepan. Bring to a boil over high heat, stirring from time to time to dissolve the sugar. When the syrup begins to boil, add the strawberries and continue to cook over high heat, stirring occasionally, until the fruit becomes translucent. Remove the pan from the heat. Take the strawberries out with a perforated spoon and put them in warmed sterilized jars. Replace the pan of syrup on the heat. Return to boiling and cook over high heat for 5 minutes. Remove from the heat, let stand for a few minutes, and pour over the strawberries, stirring lightly so that the fruit is well distributed in the jars. Cool thoroughly before sealing.

The Pyrenees

The rugged Pyrenees mountains serve not only as a political boundary between France and Spain, but also as a cultural boundary within southwestern France. The Pyrenean territory is divided among several groups of Frenchmen—Basques, Béarnais, Gascons, and Catalans—each with different customs and eating habits.

The Basques, who inhabit the extreme southwestern corner of the region, are a mysterious people. No one can say for sure where they originated, and their language cannot be related to any other language. Eating is taken seriously by the Basques, and regular competitions are held to establish who can consume the most food.

Basques are great fishermen, and cooks of the region are skilled at preparing fish. One of the triumphs of Basque cooking is *ttoro*, a rich chowder made of small fish caught off the Atlantic coast.

The pasturage is not particularly good for raising beef or dairy cattle, so Basques concentrate on raising sheep and hogs. The soil supports little besides corn (brought from America in the sixteenth century) and apples.

The gastronomic capital of the Basque country is Bayonne: its number-one specialty is ham. The celebrated *jambon de Bayonne* is raw ham cured by having Bayonne salt rubbed into it. Other specialties of Bayonne include chocolate and *pâte de cedrat*, a sweet made of a lemon-like fruit.

To the east of the Basque country is Béarn. Like the Basques, the Béarnais are trenchermen. The most famous Béarnais, King Henry IV, wished for a "chicken in every pot" for Sunday dinner. Ironically, his benevolent desire to improve his peasant's welfare led to the creation of the elaborate *poule au pot Henri IV.*

Many dishes created by the inventive Béarnais have spread throughout the Pyrenees region. The most famous of these is the *garbure*, a soup that is a meal in itself: a traditional *garbure* is so full and rich that a spoon stands in it unsupported. Although the ingredients vary, a *garbure* usually contains potatoes, beans, cabbage, poultry, ham or sausage, herbs, and spices, all put into boiling water at different times to insure that each ingredient is properly cooked and the flavors correctly blended.

There are relatively few cattle raised in the Béarn, though one of the favorite local dishes—the *estoufat*, a rich and delicious beef stew—is made from beef. Poultry and hogs are not raised on a large scale either, but almost every farmer has a few of each, and preserves made from pork, goose, duck, and turkey are favored by the peasants. Usually these preserves are prepared in goose fat, which is used in all Béarnais cooking.

As in the Basque country, sheep are raised on a large scale in the Béarn. The first concern of the Béarn sheepbreeder is the milk yield, much of which is used for making Roquefort cheese. The sheep bred for milk are also good mutton-producers, and meat from Béarn sheep is often tender enough to be cut with a spoon.

Gascony lies north and east of the Basque country and Béarn. The Gascons are symbolized by d'Artagnan, the musketeer immortalized in the Alexandre Dumas novel; and Gascon cuisine, like d'Artagnan, can be described as heroic and hardy. In much of the area the soil is poor, and only potatoes and corn are grown. A typical potato preparation is *pommes de terre à la landaise:* diced potatoes, onions, and Bayonne ham cooked in the ubiquitous goose fat. The corn, similar to American maize (Indian corn), is never eaten on the cob, but is used for cornmeal.

In the heart of Gascony is Armagnac, a region of high gastronomic excellence. The wines of the area, high in alcoholic content and rather harsh, are distilled into Armagnac brandy. Naturally, many of the dishes of the area are prepared with sauces based on this excellent brandy.

In the far eastern section of the Pyrenees region lies the country of the Catalans. The local language on both the French and Spanish sides of the Pyrenees is Catalan. On the warm shores of the Mediterranean, Catalans draw on the products of a fertile soil and a warm sea. Around Perpignan the produce is superb. Anchovies, sardines, red mullet, and lobster are the principal catches from the sea.

The cooking of the region is dominated by garlic and olive oil. Catalans often start the day by breakfasting on *el pa y all:* garlic-rubbed bread moistened with olive oil. The most famous Catalan dish is *ouillade*, a kind of soup or stew based on beans, cabbage, herbs, vegetables, and garlic. The cook then includes any pork or poultry or mutton that might be on hand. Sausages and snails are also Catalonian favorites.

The disparate and independent peoples who live in the Pyrenean region have in common their love of good food, and the cooking of southwestern France is varied and original.

Paella Basque Style

PAELLA BASQUAISE

Serves 6 to 8

½ lb. green beans
1 lb. fresh peas, shelled (about
   1 cup)
2 onions, peeled
6 tbs. oil
2 tbs. minced parsley
3 cloves garlic, peeled and
   chopped
5 slices bacon, diced
2 green sweet peppers, seeded and
   chopped
1 red hot pepper, seeded
   and chopped
1½ cups uncooked rice
4–6 large tomatoes, peeled,
   seeded, and chopped
1 tsp. saffron strands or
   ¼ tsp. powdered saffron
⅔ cup dry white wine
2 bay leaves
12 crayfish or jumbo shrimp
1½ qts. cleaned mussels
20 small chorizo or
   chipolata sausages
2 tbs. butter

This takes a long time to prepare. Consequently, it usually is eaten on Sunday in this area of France.

Bring a large pan of salted water to a boil. Add the green beans, peas, and 1 whole, peeled onion. Cook over high heat for 15 minutes. Drain the vegetables and put them to one side. Reserve the cooking liquid.

Preheat the oven to 400.

Heat the oil in a large paella pan, skillet, or saucepan. Chop the remaining onion and add it along with the parsley and garlic to the pan. Sauté gently over moderate heat for a few moments. Add the bacon and peppers to the pan and cook until they are golden. Add the rice and stir over high heat to brown. Meanwhile, reboil the reserved cooking liquid and pour enough into the pan to cover the rice by about 1 inch. Add the tomatoes along with the saffron, cooked peas, beans, salt, and pepper. Reboil, cover, and place in the preheated oven for 40 minutes or until rice is tender.

Meanwhile, heat the white wine in a saucepan with one cup of water and the bay leaves. When it boils, add the crayfish or shrimp and cook over high heat for 10 minutes. Remove the crayfish from the pan, but leave the liquid over the heat. Scrub the mussels under running water and remove the beards. Place the mussels in the boiling liquid and as soon as they are all open, remove the pan from the heat. Lift the mussels out, discarding any that haven't opened. Prick the sausages with a fork and brown them in the butter. Spoon the rice into a large heated dish. Garnish with the shellfish and the sausages.

❧

Mushrooms are plentiful on the slopes of the Pyrenees, and they are prepared in many ways. This dish is a good accompaniment for roasts or chicken.

Fried Mushrooms

CHAMPIGNONS VALLÉE D'ASPE

Serves 4

1 lb. mushrooms
⅓ cup oil
2 shallots, peeled and chopped
2 tbs. minced parsley
2 cloves garlic, crushed
5 slices bacon, chopped
1 tsp. dried thyme
juice of ½ lemon

Wipe the mushrooms clean with a damp paper towel, cut away any damaged parts, and remove the stems. Heat the oil in a skillet. Add the shallots, parsley, garlic, and bacon and sauté for a few minutes over high heat. Then add the mushrooms. Toss them by vigorously shaking the pan. Season with salt and pepper. Scatter the thyme into the skillet, sprinkle with the juice of the lemon, and serve.

Snails in Red Wine

ESCARGOTS AU VIN ROUGE

Serves 4

about 40 snails (2 small cans)
½ tsp. dried thyme
¼ cup lard
2 cloves garlic, peeled and chopped
4 shallots, peeled and chopped
¼ cup minced parsley
3 slices bacon, diced
1 tb. all-purpose flour
¾ cup red wine
4 slices white bread

Cheese Boats

BARQUETTES AU FROMAGE

Makes 24

FOR THE PASTRY:
½ cups sifted all-purpose flour
¾ cup butter, cut into small pieces
3 tbs. water
1 egg, beaten, for glazing

FOR THE FILLING:
4 eggs
¼ lb. Urt or Swiss cheese, thinly sliced
½ cup butter, cut into small pieces
pinch of cayenne pepper
⅔ cup dry white wine

The people of Burgundy prepare their snails in the oven with butter and garlic. In the Pyrenees, snails are often grilled with bacon on a sheet of slate over a wood fire, or they are prepared in the following way.

Wash and drain the snails and sprinkle them with thyme. Heat the lard in a skillet and lightly sauté the garlic, shallots, and parsley. Add the bacon. As soon as the mixture is golden, sprinkle with flour and stir for 2 or 3 minutes. Gradually add the red wine, stirring well. Lower the heat, cover and cook gently for 15 minutes. Add the snails, stir, and season with salt and pepper. Cook gently for 5 minutes. Toast the bread and arrange it on a serving plate. Pour the snails and sauce over the toast and serve immediately.

❧

This hot first course can be served equally well as an hors d'oeuvre with cocktails. Traditionally, cheese from Urt in the Basse Pyrenees is used, but a salty cheese of the Swiss Gruyère variety is quite suitable.

To prepare the pastry, measure the flour into a bowl and make a well in the center. Add a pinch of salt and ½ cup of butter. Working quickly with your fingertips, blend the mixture until it resembles coarse oatmeal. Add the water, mix, and knead lightly to a dough. Shape the dough into a ball, cover with a cloth, and let rest in a cool place.

For the filling, mix the eggs in a saucepan. Add the cheese, butter, and cayenne pepper. Finally, add the white wine. Place the pan over low heat and cook, stirring constantly with a wooden spoon, until the mixture is evenly thickened. Do not boil.

Preheat the oven to 400.

Roll out the dough on a floured board. Grease 24 small oval molds or round muffin tins with ¼ cup of butter. Line them with the dough. With the tines of a fork, prick the dough at the base of each mold. Bake in the preheated oven for 8 minutes and remove. Brush the surface of each with the beaten egg to glaze the pastry and help it brown. Return the molds to the oven for 2 to 3 minutes. Remove the molds and lower the oven to 350. Fill the pastries with the cheese mixture and return to the oven for 10 minutes or until the filling is golden brown. Serve hot.

This highly seasoned first course is relatively unknown outside this area of France.

Remove and discard the outside leaves of the artichokes. Split the artichokes in half (or into quarters if they are large) and remove the choke. Sprinkle all the cut surfaces with lemon juice.

Heat the oil in a heavy skillet and sauté the shallot, garlic, and parsley for a few moments. Cut the anchovy fillets into small pieces and add them, with the pieces of artichoke, olives, and white wine, to the pan. Add a good grinding of pepper but do not add salt as the anchovies are already salted. Cover and simmer for 1½ hours over low heat. Serve hot or cold.

Braised Artichokes

ARTICHAUTS RAMUNTCHO

Serves 6

12 small globe artichokes or
   6 large ones
juice of 1 lemon
6 tbs. olive oil
1 shallot, peeled and chopped
2 cloves garlic, chopped
2 tbs. minced parsley
6 anchovy fillets in oil
12 pitted green olives
¾ cup dry white wine

Braised Goose

OIE EN DAUBE

Serves 6 to 8

2 lbs. fresh chestnuts or 4 cups of
  whole, canned, unsweetened
  chestnuts
2 tbs. sugar
2 tbs. butter
1 goose liver
few leaves fresh, or
  2 tsps. dried sage
1 7-lb. oven-ready goose
20 slices bacon
1 bottle dry white wine
9 tbs. Cognac
5 peppercorns
pinch of nutmeg
2 tbs. each chopped fresh parsley,
  thyme, and sage or
  ½ tsp. each dried
1 calf's foot or foreshank

This cold dish is prepared in advance for special occasions such as Christmas Eve. If your goose is frozen, defrost it overnight in the refrigerator or in a pan of running water.

If using fresh chestnuts, slash them and boil for 15 minutes; then shell and skin them completely. If canned chestnuts are used, rinse them under cold running water and dry them in a cloth.

Sprinkle the prepared chestnuts with sugar. Heat the butter in a skillet and brown the chestnuts and the goose liver. Season with salt and the sage. Stuff the goose with this mixture, sew up the opening with strong white thread, and truss (see illustration pp. 88-89).

Line a shallow roasting pan with the bacon slices. Place the goose on top and add the white wine and Cognac. Season with salt. Add the peppercorns, nutmeg, herbs, and, finally, the calf's foot. Cover with a tight-fitting lid and cook for 15 minutes over high heat; reduce the heat to low and continue braising for 2½ to 3 hours.

Remove the stuffing and carve the goose. Arrange both on a deep-sided serving dish. Strain the liquid from the pan into a bowl and place it uncovered in the refrigerator. When the sauce is quite cold the fat will rise to the surface and can easily be removed. After the fat is removed, reduce the sauce and pour it over the goose and stuffing. Leave the dish in a cool place until the sauce sets to a firm jelly.

❦

Open Omelet

PIPÉRADE

Serves 2

3 green sweet peppers
½ small chili (optional)
1 medium onion, peeled and
  chopped (¾ cup)
2 cloves garlic, peeled and
  chopped
2 tbs. minced parsley
4 medium tomatoes, peeled,
  seeded, and chopped
¼ cup oil
4 eggs
¼ cup goose fat or bacon fat
4 slices bacon

This combination of eggs, green peppers, and tomatoes is frequently served as a first course in the Basque country.

Trim and seed the peppers. Slice the flesh into small strips. Do the same with the chili. Place them in a large bowl with the onion, garlic, parsley, and tomatoes. Heat the oil in a small skillet, add the vegetables, and sauté gently over low heat for 5 minutes, stirring occasionally. Meanwhile, beat the eggs with a pinch of salt. Heat the goose or bacon fat in a skillet and pour in the beaten eggs, shaking the pan so they spread evenly. Allow the eggs to just set over high heat, and then immediately pour the vegetable mixture on top. Lower the heat and stir briskly with a wooden spoon, as if scrambling eggs, but more quickly. Cook for less than 1 minute. The eggs must be cooked but still moist. Transfer to a heated dish. Lightly fry the bacon slices, arrange them on top of the pipérade, and serve immediately.

Duck Pâté

PÂTÉ DE CANARD EN
TERRINE

Serves 6 to 8

1 2½-lb. duck
2 tbs. butter
pinch of nutmeg
¾–1 lb. fatback or blanched salt
  pork, cut into strips
1½ lbs. ground lean pork
2 tbs. minced parsley
1 tsp. dried sage
1 egg, beaten
½ lb. sliced smoked ham
  (Virginia, for example)
⅓ cup Cognac

Pâtés can be made in almost
any kind of dish from the special oval or rectangular mold
called a *terrine*, to a loaf pan or
a soufflé dish. Well wrapped, a
pâté will keep in the refrigerator for 10 days or more.

---

*Either a wild duckling or a domestic bird may be used for
this recipe. It is better to choose a duck that is not too fat. In
France, for example, the Barbary ducks are preferred to the
ones from Nantes for this pâté.*

Preheat the oven to 475.

After the duck has been plucked, singed, and cleaned (reserve the liver for another dish), rub it with butter and roast
it for about 1 hour. Lower the oven to 400. When finished,
bone, skin, and slice the meat, which should still be slightly
rosy. Set aside the breast meat, and grind the rest. Sprinkle with salt, pepper, and nutmeg. Mix together the ground
duck flesh and ground pork, parsley, sage, and beaten egg.
Line the bottom and sides of an ovenproof terrine or loaf
pan with half the strips of fatback or salt pork. In alternate
layers add the ground-meat mixture and then the sliced
smoked ham and the sliced breast meat from the duck.
Sprinkle with the Cognac. Cover with the remainder of the
fatback or salt pork strips. Place the terrine in a pan containing about 1 inch of boiling water. Set in the oven for 15
minutes; then lower the heat to 250 and cook for 3½ hours.
Let the pâté cool with a weight on top at room temperature
and then chill. Serve cold in the earthenware dish.

❧

Sweet and Sour Ham

JAMBON À
L'AIGRE-DOUCE

Serves 4

¼ cup olive oil
3 tbs. minced parsley
2 shallots, peeled and chopped
4 thick slices prosciutto or
  other raw ham
3 tbs. honey
6 tbs. wine vinegar
pinch of nutmeg

*This recipe from the region of Cerdagne dates from the Mid-
dle Ages. The combination of sweet and sour flavors was
greatly enjoyed in festive dishes.*

Heat the oil in a skillet, add the parsley and shallots, and
sauté for a moment over high heat. Add the slices of prosciutto or ham and cook them quickly, turning once with a
spatula. Remove the ham to a heated serving dish. Add the
honey, wine vinegar, and nutmeg to the skillet. Heat for
half a minute over moderate heat, stirring well with a
wooden spoon. Pour the sauce over the ham and serve.

The Pyrenees

Brook or river trout are the most suitable for this easily pre-pared dish. Their flesh is white and delicate, their skin a bright blue.

Preheat the oven to 400.

Place a sprig of fresh thyme (or ¼ teaspoon dried) inside each trout. Sprinkle with a little lemon juice, and wrap each trout in a slice of bacon.

Grease each sheet of foil with a quarter of the butter. Completely enclose each fish in a sheet of the foil, greased side to the fish. Arrange on a baking dish and bake for 10 minutes. Lower the oven heat to 350 and bake for an additional 10 minutes. Serve the trout in their foil packages.

Baked Trout

TRUITES EN PAPILLOTE

Serves 4

4 small trout, cleaned, washed, and
    dried
4 sprigs fresh, or 1 tsp. dried thyme
juice of 1 lemon
4 thin slices lean bacon
4 sheets aluminum foil
3 tbs. butter

Chicken in the Pot

POULE AU POT HENRI IV

Serves 6 to 8

1 4–4½ lb. oven-ready
   chicken

FOR THE STUFFING:
2 tbs. butter
1 chicken liver
4½ cups fresh bread crumbs,
   lightly packed
10 slices lean bacon
2 eggs, beaten
1 clove garlic, peeled and
   chopped
few sprigs parsley
5 tbs. Cognac

FOR THE STOCK POT:
3 qts. of water
1 leek
1 celery stalk
4 small carrots
4 turnips
1 large onion, peeled and
   stuck with 3 cloves
4 peppercorns
bouquet garni

Henry IV, one of the most popular kings in the history of France, was a native of Béarn. He wanted his subjects "to put a chicken in the cooking pot every Sunday" as a sign of prosperity.

First prepare the stuffing for the chicken. Melt the butter in a skillet, add the chicken liver, and brown it. Place the liver in a mixing bowl and mash it with the bread crumbs. Finely chop the bacon and add it, along with the beaten eggs, garlic, parsley, Cognac, salt, and pepper. Mix well and stuff the chicken with the mixture. Sew up the opening with strong white thread and truss (see illustration pp. 88-89).

Heat the water in a large pot (ideally, an earthenware pot protected from the heat by an asbestos mat). Peel, trim, and wash the leek. Trim and wash the celery, carrots, and turnips. Add the onion and the vegetables to the pot, with the bouquet garni, salt, and peppercorns. Bring to a boil and add the chicken. Simmer for 1½ hours.

Discard the onion stuck with cloves and the bouquet garni. Place vegetables from the poule au pot on a platter. Serve the chicken separately, with rice or boiled potatoes.

The broth will be quite greasy. Put it in the refrigerator to cool. The fat will rise to the surface and is easily removed. Serve the soup at a later meal.

This is an excellent method for cooking a "stewing fowl"—a polite term for the hen that is almost a year old and losing some of her efficiency and energy as an egg-producer. It is good value both in terms of per-pound cost and taste. The older flesh is rich in flavor that is often lacking in younger chickens. The long cooking with the vegetables softens the bird and produces a delicious chicken as well as a rich and flavorful broth. Look for a stewing hen that has a broad breast and plenty of yellow fat showing through the skin.

Almond Candy

TOURON

Makes about 1 dozen

1¼ cups finely ground almonds
1 cup sugar
3 tbs. all-purpose flour
1 tsp. finely grated lemon peel
2 egg whites

In the Pyrenees the word touron *is used to describe several confections. According to the region, it may mean a flaky almond cake, a type of nougat, or, as here, almond candy.*

Preheat the oven to 350.

Mix together the almonds and sugar. Add 2 tablespoons of flour and then the grated lemon peel. Mix thoroughly. Beat the egg whites with a pinch of salt until they are stiff and gently fold them into the dry ingredients. Dust a flat baking sheet with 1 tablespoon of flour; then spoon on the touron paste. Using a spatula, spread the paste smoothly and thinly. Cover with a sheet of foil, oiled on the side next to the touron. Bake in the center of the preheated oven for 20 minutes. The touron should be dry on the outside but soft in the middle. Let it cool before cutting into rectangles, 2 inches by 1 inch.

Flamed Jam Omelet

OMELETTE FLAMBÉE

Serves 4

4 eggs
2 tbs. butter
½ cup jam or marmalade
6 tbs. confectioners sugar
⅓ cup Cointreau, Grand
    Marnier, or curaçao

This is an extremely simple dessert. It is nothing more than a sweet, jam-filled omelet, sprinkled with liqueur, and flamed before serving.

Break the eggs into a large bowl and beat vigorously with a fork for about 1 minute. Heat the butter in an omelet pan, shaking the skillet until the butter is very hot but not brown. (Sometimes a teaspoon of oil is added, which allows the butter to reach a higher temperature without burning.) Then pour the beaten eggs into the skillet, all at once, and shake the pan while keeping it over the heat. The great chefs cook the omelet without touching it with a fork, only shaking the skillet and tilting it to spread the eggs and ensure even cooking. However, this needs a strong arm, so most home cooks use a fork. As soon as the border of the omelet is cooked, raise it, and the uncooked egg will run from the center to the edge. As soon as this new border is cooked, raise the border again and so on until the whole base of the omelet has thickened but is not dry. The whole operation takes only 2 to 3 minutes over high heat. Remove the skillet from the heat. Spread the jam or marmalade on the middle of the omelet. Then flip the omelet onto a heated plate, folding it in half. Sift the sugar over the omelet and pour over the slightly warmed liqueur. Turning your face away, ignite the alcohol with a match, and carry it to the table, having first turned off the lights.

Raise the cooked borders with a fork.

Spread with jam, or other filling.

Flip onto plate, folding in half.

One of the secrets of a successful omelet is the pan you use and the care you give it. A French omelet pan is generally made of plain iron or heavy aluminum. A nonstick skillet is not recommended. The pan should be treated before you use it. Heat it for a moment and put in a teaspoon of butter. Remove the skillet from the heat and rub the inside with soft paper toweling. If the pan is used only for omelets, it is never washed but rather wiped carefully after each use with paper toweling.

This recipe invites many variations. The omelet can be filled with bananas which have been sugared and cooked briefly in butter; use rum for the flaming. Another successful combination is a filling of strawberry jam and the flaming with strawberry liqueur; or, use apple jam and set the omelet alight with Calvados. Be careful to use combinations that go well together. The alcohol must be strong enough to burn easily; the best spirits are those which combine concentrated flavor with high proof, such as brandy or rum.

Languedoc

For centuries the Languedoc has been a center of fine provincial cooking (haute cuisine is practically unknown here). Its produce is superb, and its cooking extremely hearty and tasty.

As the region produces great recipes, it also produces great cooks and restaurateurs. One of the most enterprising was Prosper Montagne, a native of the Languedoc, who probably did more than anyone else to bring the region's recipes to the attention of the world. His writings on provincial cooking and his famed restaurant in Paris placed special emphasis on the native excellence of Languedoc's cuisine. Another, Auguste Colombie, started in nineteenth century Paris, the first school of cooking for young ladies. He emphasized recipes of Languedoc and chic Parisian students were introduced to the earthy cooking of the province.

Probably the most characteristic dish of Languedoc is *cassoulet*, which consists of beans and meats. The people of each town claim to have the best recipe for it, and its composition varies with the cook as well as with the ingredients that are available. Some combine the beans with fresh pork, ham, pork shoulder, sausage or pork cracklings. Others include all these ingredients plus chunks of mutton leg, partridge, bacon, preserved goose, or duck. Also added to the pot is goose fat, seasoning, herbs, an onion studded with cloves, garlic, and a liquid such as meat bouillon.

The Mediterranean yields oysters, lobster, and tuna. Poultry and game birds are also abundant. Geese are plentiful, and the goose-liver pâté is breathtakingly enhanced by the addition of the famed Languedoc truffle.

The long, fat Toulouse sausage is another specialty of the region. It can be served as an hors d'oeuvre or prepared as a main dish. Mutton and lamb are plentiful and are prepared in a number of ways. Many braised beef dishes are based upon the highly esteemed flavor of the cattle raised in the region.

Melted ham or goose fat, used widely at one time, has been replaced by butter. Olive groves are plentiful, but only a small amount of olive oil is used in cooking. The olives are eaten in their natural state or *à la picholine* (preserved in salt).

Pâtés of all kinds are popular: the hare pâté from St. Agrève, the wild-rabbit pâté from Afrons, mutton pâtés from Nîmes, and unusual, delicious little pâtes of sugared meat from Béziers. The recipes for all of these date back at least a thousand years, and are as traditional to the area as Thanksgiving turkey is to the United States.

As in many of the other regions, each town has its own special delicacy: in Toulouse, real violets crystallized in sugar; in Castres, nougat candies; in Montpellier, homemade chocolates; in Carcassone, crystallized fruits, especially the *marrons glacés;* in Albi, cookies called *navattes*, made with preserved fruits and spices; and in Uzès, black licorice candy.

The Languedoc is the largest wine-growing area in France. It produces about 45 percent of French wines, though few are well-known abroad. Although they cannot be ranked with the more famous château- and estate-bottled wines, they have a character and use of their own, and are enjoyed for their freshness and clarity. A bottle or carafe of *vin ordinaire* deliciously complements a provincial dinner.

Perhaps the best dry rosé in all of France comes from Tavel, a tiny village on the slopes of the Rhone Valley. Only about 200,000 cases are produced each year, and woodlands in the area with the proper red, stony, sandy soil are being converted to vineyards in an effort to keep up with the demand for this wine. Tavel rosé is a blend of various white and black grapes, primarily Grenache. The skins of the pressed grapes remain in the vats for only one night, just long enough to give the wine its beautiful orangy-pink color. It is a wine of great character and balance with a wonderful bouquet that should be drunk young and well-chilled and goes well with almost any food. Tavel rosé is greatly appreciated by connoisseurs.

Other wines of the Languedoc region are Minervois, Carigan, Gaillac, and the delicate wine of Frontignan, which is especially delicious drunk before the entrée or with dessert. Many of the less-known wines are pleasant to drink every day, and do not have a very high alcoholic content. Perrier, one of France's best-known table waters, comes from natural springs in Languedoc.

Gastronomically, the province is fortunate with its good wines, excellent produce, fine meats, poultry, fish, and desserts.

Pork and Bean Casserole

CASSOULET TOULOUSAIN

Serves 12

FOR THE BEANS:

2 lbs. dry white beans, such as
    Great Northern
¾ lb. breast of salt pork
½ lb. fresh pork rind
1 small carrot, peeled
1 large onion, peeled and stuck
    with 4 cloves
bouquet garni
¼ cup goose fat, lard, or bacon fat
4 cloves garlic, peeled

FOR THE MEAT:

1 lb. boned shoulder of lamb
1 lb. boned loin of pork
¼ cup goose fat, lard, or bacon fat
1 large onion, peeled and chopped
3 cloves garlic, crushed
5 tomatoes, peeled, seeded, juiced,
    and chopped
1 cup beef stock or canned beef
    bouillon
bouquet garni

FOR THE GARNISH:

½–¾ lb. Toulouse garlic sausage or
    well seasoned cooked sausage
2 pieces preserved goose (optional)
¾ cup toasted bread crumbs
6 tbs. goose fat, lard, or bacon fat

Cassoulet invites endless variation, and you should use your instinct and imagination to make additions or substitutions. The preparation of this hearty dish can be spread over several days.

Soak the beans in a bowl of cold water for 3 hours or overnight. Drain. Put the beans into an earthenware pot protected from the heat by an asbestos mat, or into a large casserole. Add the salt pork, pork rind, carrot, onion, bouquet garni, the fat, and the garlic. Add water just to cover the beans. Cover the casserole and bring to a boil. Lower the heat and simmer gently, so that the beans do not burst. Cook for 2½ hours, stirring gently from time to time and adding a little more water, if necessary, to keep the beans covered.

While the beans are cooking, brown the shoulder of lamb and loin of pork in the goose fat in a large skillet. Drain and put the meat into another large pan, setting aside the skillet for browning the sausage later. Season the meat with salt and pepper. Add the onion, garlic, and tomatoes to the pan containing the meat. Moisten with the stock and a little water. Add the bouquet garni and simmer, covered, for 2 to 2½ hours.

Preheat the oven to 300.

Cut the sausage into large slices and brown it in the same skillet in which the lamb and pork were browned. Remove and discard the salt pork and pork rind from the beans. Cut the meat into serving pieces and alternate layers of beans and meat in a large, deep casserole. Finish with a layer of the optional preserved goose and the sausage slices, pushing them down gently into the beans if necessary. Sprinkle with bread crumbs. Dot with the remaining fat, and set the casserole into a large roasting pan half filled with hot water. Place in preheated oven and cook for at least 45 minutes. Serve very hot from the casserole.

Cheese Soup

SOUPE AU FROMAGE

Serves 4

4 cloves garlic (or to taste)
4½ cups water
4 white peppercorns
pinch of nutmeg
¼ lb. Cantal cheese
¼ lb. Swiss cheese
approximately 15 slices of French
  bread
¼ cup olive oil
1 tsp. dried thyme

If the hard, strong Cantal cheese called for in this recipe is unavailable, you can substitute Port Salut or Edam.

To prepare garlic stock, peel the cloves of garlic and put them into a saucepan with the water, peppercorns, nutmeg, and a pinch of salt. Bring to a boil, lower the heat and simmer for 30 minutes. During this time cut the cheeses into very thin slices (a knife dipped into boiling water cuts more finely).

In a covered casserole, arrange a layer of bread slices, a layer of cheese, a tablespoon of oil, and ¼ teaspoon of thyme. Continue doing this with the remaining cheese, bread, and thyme. Then moisten gradually with the garlic stock. Cover the casserole and simmer gently for 30 minutes.

Spinach Tartlets

TARTELETTES AUX ÉPINARDS

Makes 2 to 3 dozen

FOR THE PASTRY:
1¾ cups sifted all-purpose flour
½ cup butter
1 egg

FOR THE FILLING:
2 lbs. fresh spinach or
  1 package frozen spinach
½ cup candied orange peel
1 tsp. sugar
1 tb. orange-flower water or
  a few drops almond extract
¼ cup finely ground almonds

These tartlets, an unusual first course, should be served hot. They may be made in advance and reheated.

Measure the sifted flour for the pastry into a bowl. Add the butter in small pieces, a pinch of salt, and the egg. Mix together; then quickly rub the pastry between your fingers. Knead it and shape it into a ball. Wrap in a floured cloth and put the dough in a cool place to rest.

Meanwhile, if using fresh spinach, wash it and place in a saucepan of 1 or 2 tablespoons of boiling salted water. Cover the pan and cook over moderate heat for 15 minutes. If using frozen spinach, cook as directed on the package. Drain, squeeze out all the moisture, and chop. Return the spinach to the saucepan. Dice the candied orange peel and add it to the spinach along with the sugar, orange-flower water or almond extract, and ground almonds. Mix well.

Preheat the oven to 400.

Roll out the pastry thinly on a floured board. Cut 3-inch circles using a cookie cutter or floured rim of a glass or cup pressed down on the pastry and trimmed with a pointed knife. Place a teaspoon of spinach mixture in the center of each circle. Fold the pastry in half so that you have a semicircle. Press the sides together with your fingertips and prick the pastry with a fork on the rounded side of each tartlet. Place on a greased cookie sheet and bake 10 to 15 minutes.

This recipe was provided by Monsieur Barrière, the head chef at the Grand Hôtel et Tivollier *in Toulouse. It is named after a great lady of fourteenth-century Toulouse.*

Preheat the oven to 350.

Wipe the duckling and prepare the stuffing. Add the olives to a saucepan of boiling salted water and simmer for 5 minutes to soften them. Then drain. Remove the skins from the sausages, slice them into rounds, or cut into pieces. Mix the garlic, sausage, and olives. Heat a third of the butter in a skillet, add the duck liver, and brown lightly. Crush the liver and add it to the stuffing.

Stuff the duckling with the mixture and sew up the opening with strong white thread and truss (see illustration pp. 88-89). Roast on a spit or place the duckling on a rack in a roasting pan and place in the preheated oven. Basting occasionally with the pan juices, cook for about 1 hour on the electric spit, or 1¼ hours in the oven.

Toward the end of the cooking time, heat the remaining butter in a skillet and brown the bread, turning occasionally. Lightly season the cooked duckling and cut it into serving portions. Arrange the duckling pieces on the sautéed bread on a hot serving dish, with the stuffing on the top. Pour off the fat for future use. To the meat drippings in the roasting pan (or pan underneath the spit), add wine, season with salt and pepper, and bring almost to a boil, stirring constantly with a wooden spoon. Pour the sauce over the duckling and serve immediately.

This dish is most delicious when made with young, fresh, tender beans. If you use frozen beans, cook them for only 5 minutes.

Rinse and drain the beans. Heat the butter in a large saucepan and sauté the bacon. Add the beans and cook them for a moment over high heat. Cover, reduce heat, and continue to cook for 25 minutes, shaking the pan frequently. Add the parsley and garlic to the pan. Sprinkle with the flour, and season with salt and pepper. Add the savory and the water or stock. Cook very gently for 45 minutes. Just before serving, stir in the egg yolks and heat very gently, but do not boil. Serve on a heated dish.

Stuffed Duckling

CANETON CLÉMENCE ISAURE

Serves 4

1 3½-lb. oven-ready duckling

FOR THE STUFFING:
½ cup pitted green olives
3 Toulouse sausages, or
    other cooked sausages
5 cloves garlic, crushed
6 tbs. butter
liver of the duckling
4 slices white bread, diced
¾ cup dry white wine

Creamed Beans

FÈVES SAINTE-ENIMIE

Serves 4

1⅓ cups shelled fava or lima beans
2 tbs. butter or lard
¼ lb. Canadian bacon, diced
2 tbs. minced parsley
3 cloves garlic, crushed
1 tb. all-purpose flour
few sprigs fresh savory
1 cup water or stock
3 egg yolks

Shad with Sorrel and Bacon

ALOSE D'AURÉLIE

Serves 4

1 2-lb. shad, cleaned and boned
6 tbs. butter
3 tbs. olive oil
1 onion, peeled and finely chopped
  (½–¾ cup)
4 slices bacon
pinch of sugar
¾ cup dry white wine
1 lb. sorrel or spinach
juice of 1 lemon

Shad is a particularly delicious and delicate fish, generally available in spring. Ask your fishmonger to bone it for you, as it is a tedious procedure.

Wash and dry the shad. Make shallow incisions all over with the point of a knife. In a small saucepan, melt 2 tablespoons of the butter with the oil and coat the fish with this.

Melt 2 more tablespoons of butter in a skillet and sauté the onion over moderate heat for 5 minutes. Add the shad. This step is only to brown the fish on both sides and not to cook it—5 minutes is sufficient.

Arrange 2 large slices of bacon in the bottom of a heavy skillet and place the shad and onions on top. Season lavishly with salt and pepper. Dot with the remaining butter and sprinkle with sugar. Begin to cook over high heat and, when the bacon starts to melt, pour the wine into the pan.

Wash and dry the sorrel or spinach. Chop it coarsely and add it to the pan, to cover the fish. Put the remaining bacon slices on top, cover, and continue to cook for 2 hours over low heat. Just before serving, sprinkle with the lemon juice.

❧

Stuffed Eggplant

AUBERGINES FARCIES

Serves 4

4 medium eggplants
4 cups white bread crumbs, lightly
  packed
⅓ cup milk
pinch of nutmeg
2 cloves garlic, peeled and
  chopped
1¼ lb. mushrooms, chopped
  coarsely
4 tbs. minced parsley
½ lb. cooked ham, finely chopped
6 tbs. toasted bread crumbs
⅓ cup olive oil

Eggplant is greatly appreciated in Languedoc, where it is cooked in many different ways. This preparation is very popular and goes well with roasts and poultry. It can also be served as a separate vegetable dish.

Preheat the oven to 350.

Cut the end off each eggplant and split in half lengthways without peeling. Scoop out the seeds. Sprinkle the cut surface of the eggplants with salt and leave for 20 minutes to draw out the moisture.

For the stuffing, soak the bread crumbs in the milk for a moment. Add the nutmeg, garlic, mushrooms, parsley, and ham. Season with pepper.

Rinse the eggplants under cold running water and dry them. Arrange them in a lightly greased baking dish. Top with the stuffing and sprinkle with the toasted bread crumbs. Dribble the olive oil on top. Bake 45 minutes to 1 hour in the preheated oven. Serve in the baking dish.

This delicious, classic stew is popular all over France. A combination of cuts of veal from the breast, shoulder, neck, and rump is traditional for this stew. They are cartilaginous, however, and you may prefer using the boned leg or rump.

Put the meat into a saucepan and cover with wine and water. Add the veal bone (which gives flavor), salt and pepper to taste, onion, carrots, garlic, and the bouquet garni. Cover and cook over moderate heat for about 40 minutes, skimming continually to remove the gray-brown substance which will rise to the surface.

Remove the meat and vegetables and put them on a plate. Discard the bone, the onion stuck with cloves, and the bouquet garni. Strain the stock and reserve 1¼ cups. Melt the butter and, as soon as it foams, add the flour and stir vigorously for about a minute. Gradually stir in the strained stock. Add the meat and vegetables, and the mushrooms. Cook for an additional 20 minutes. Mix the cream with the egg yolks and lemon juice in the serving dish. Stir a few tablespoons of the cooking liquid into this mixture and, when it is bound together, add the remainder of the stew.

Veal Stew

BLANQUETTE DE VEAU

Serves 4

2 lbs. lean boneless veal, cut into
　2-inch cubes
⅔ cup dry white wine
1 large veal bone, split
1 medium onion, peeled and
　stuck with 4 cloves
6 small carrots, thickly sliced
2 cloves garlic, crushed
bouquet garni
2 tbs. butter
3 tbs. all-purpose flour
¼ lb. small mushrooms, wiped
　clean
½ cup heavy cream
3 egg yolks
juice of 1 lemon

> In the Midi, cream isn't used and pitted green olives are added to enhance the flavor.

❧

There is a legend that Roquefort cheese was made popular by the Emperor Charlemagne. For a successful salad, it is essential that the lettuce be absolutely bone-dry. You might keep a large towel in your kitchen reserved for drying lettuce.

Wash the chicory under cold running water, strip off the leaves by hand, one by one (break large leaves in half), and dry well. Rub the inside of a salad bowl with the garlic and discard the clove. Place the walnuts in the bowl, add the Roquefort cheese, and blend them together. Gradually mix in the cream and the lemon juice. Then add the oil, mixing thoroughly with a wooden spoon or beating lightly with a whisk. Add the chicory and mix until it is thoroughly coated with the salad dressing.

Salad with Roquefort Dressing

SALADE AU ROQUEFORT

Serves 4

1 head chicory
1 clove garlic, peeled
1 cup shelled walnuts, chopped
¼-½ lb. Roquefort cheese
½ cup heavy cream
juice of 1 lemon
6 tbs. walnut or peanut oil

Chestnut Pudding

FLAN CÉVENOL

Serves 4

1½ lbs. fresh chestnuts or
   1 lb. canned whole chestnuts
½ cup butter
1 cup milk
½ vanilla bean or
   2–3 drops vanilla extract
1 cup sugar
4 eggs, separated
½ cup sifted confectioners sugar
½ cup heavy cream, whipped and
   flavored with ¼ teaspoon vanilla
   (optional)

Vanilla Cream Pie

TARTE À LA CRÈME

Serves 6

FOR THE PUFF PASTRY:
2 cups sifted all-purpose flour
¾ cup ice water
¾ cup plus 2 tbs. chilled butter
milk, for glazing

FOR THE PASTRY CREAM:
1 cup milk
½ vanilla bean or
   2–3 drops vanilla extract
grated peel of 1 orange
¾ cup sugar
5 tbs. all-purpose flour
3 egg yolks
2 tbs. butter

This is a substantial dessert, particularly good in winter.

If using fresh chestnuts, slash them and cook them for 15 minutes in boiling salted water. Strain and remove the outside shell and the skin. Return the chestnuts to the pan, cover again with boiling water, and simmer for 30 minutes, or until they are tender. If using canned chestnuts, simply drain and rinse them thoroughly; then drain again.

Preheat the oven to 350.

Pass the chestnuts through a sieve or food mill to make a puree. Cut the butter into small pieces, add it, and mix well.

Place the vanilla bean or extract in the milk and bring to a boil in a saucepan. Discard the bean and pour the hot milk slowly over the chestnut mixture, stirring it in gradually. Mix in the sugar and egg yolks. Beat the egg whites with a pinch of salt until they are stiff. Then fold them gently into the mixture.

Thoroughly butter a 6-cup soufflé dish and pour in the mixture. Bake for 30 minutes. Chill the pudding completely before unmolding, and then sprinkle with confectioners sugar. Serve as it is or cover with the whipped cream.

❧

This is a Sunday dish in France, either bought at the cake shop after church or prepared at home on the previous day.

To make the puff pastry, sift the flour in a heap on a floured board and make a well in the center. Into this well pour the ice water and a pinch of salt. Knead lightly with your fingertips and form the pastry into a ball. Let it rest, covered, for 30 minutes in the refrigerator.

After 30 minutes, roll the pastry into a large circle. Scatter small pieces of butter in the middle of this circle and fold the pastry to enclose the butter, as if making a parcel. Sprinkle with flour and roll out very lightly into a long narrow rectangle. The pieces of butter will stick out. Bring the bottom third up and the top third down, as if folding a long letter. Turn it a quarter of the way around. Roll out again into a long, narrow rectangle, sprinkle with flour, and again fold it 3 times. Let it rest in the refrigerator for 20 minutes. Repeat the process; that is, roll the pastry into a long, narrow rectangle, fold it three times, and repeat twice, turning the pastry a quarter of way around each time after folding. Let it rest again for 20 minutes. Begin the process again. In France, this is called giving 6 turns to the pastry. Proceed with the recipe during the final resting.

Preheat the oven to 400.

Grease an 8- or 9-inch tart mold or pie plate and line it with the puff pastry. Prick the pastry with a fork so that it rises evenly. Brush the edges with milk and bake in the preheated oven for 12 minutes.

Preheat the broiler.

Meanwhile, prepare the pastry cream. Heat the milk with the vanilla bean or vanilla extract and the grated orange peel. Mix ½ cup of the sugar with the flour in a saucepan. Add the egg yolks and gradually stir in the hot milk mixture. Cook over low heat for about 5 minutes, stirring constantly with a spoon or whisk until the mixture thickens. Remove the pan from the heat and take out the vanilla bean. Cut the butter into small pieces and stir it in. Pour this thick cream mixture into the pastry shell. Sprinkle with the remaining ¼ cup of sugar. Broil quickly until the sugar melts and caramelizes. Serve warm, if possible, but do not reheat.

An efficient way to remove just the peel (zest) and none of the bitter white pith from citrus fruit is to use a vegetable peeler with a swivel blade. Strip the zest off the fruit with the peeler and then chop it finely with a sharp knife. It is a superior method to grating because it saves the knuckles and the bitterness produced by the pith is eliminated.

Massif Central

It is often said that the Massif Central is literally the heart of France; here, in the middle of the map, scattered French Gallic tribes first ceased fighting each other, uniting under one standard to repulse Caesar's legions.

The Massif Central is comprised of three distinct areas: Bourbonnais, a pleasant country of gently rolling hills and valleys, full of fruit and vegetable gardens and lakes well stocked with carp and pike; Limousin, a vast parkland where cattle graze, and picturesque châteaux are surrounded by acres of cherry orchards; and Auvergne, land of mountains and swift-flowing rivers. Here sheep feed on scented herbs that give their flesh a delicate flavor; salmon and trout leap in the clear streams; and natural, healing springs bubble up from the volcanic soil. Bottles of this natural mineral water are sold all over Europe.

The cooking of the Auvergnats is similar in spirit to the type found in most mountainous regions: satisfying and tasty, but prepared simply and without great sophistication. Northern Auvergne produces fine grain, such vegetables as potatoes, lentils, peas, and mushrooms, and a variety of fruits—cherries, peaches, strawberries, apples, apricots, and pears. Excellent chestnuts and walnuts grow in the area, which is well known also for its superb pork, ham, cattle, sheep, and fish.

The characteristic dishes of the Auvergne are exemplary of a region making full use of its raw ingredients. They include *tripoux*, stuffed sheep's feet, *fricondeaux*, a pork pâté, *friands de Saint-Flour*, sausage meat pâtés rolled in leaves, *tourte à la viande*, chopped pork and veal in a pastry shell. Potato dishes are plentiful; chief amongst them is *truffade*, mashed or fried potatoes usually prepared with cheese, cabbage, or pork.

Pommes de terre au lard, another typical Auvergne potato dish, includes diced bacon and small onions.

Pastry is popular in the area: *cornets* (cones filled with heavy cream), *bourriolles* (sweet pancakes of buckwheat flour), *picoussel* (sweet buckwheat-flour pancakes filled with plums and seasoned with herbs). There are also some famous cheeses, many of which are used in cooking: Saint-Nectaire, Grand Mural, Fourme, Gaperon, Pelardon de Ruoms, and the recently developed and very popular Bleu d'Auvergne. No great wines are produced in the Auvergne. Perhaps this accounts for the fact that a favored Auvergnat drink is *gaspo*—buttermilk—which is drunk with meals.

The Limousin region also produces fine raw materials. Many of the dishes of this region consist of grain, fruits, nuts, eggs, beef, mushrooms, and game. Limousin has excellent pasturage, which accounts for its fine cattle. Superior pigs are raised here as well, and pork is an important part of the Limousin cuisine. Probably the most popular pork dish is *carré de porc à la limousine*: roast pork with red cabbage and chestnuts. It is impossible to consider the cooking of Limousin without thinking of *lièvre à la royale*, a hare dish with elaborate stuffing. Soups are especially typical of the region: boiled oats soup, one made from rye bread, and cabbage soup. *Farcidure*, a little ball of stuffing made from buckwheat flour, sorrel, and beets enclosed in cabbage leaves, is eaten throughout Limousin. Meat pâtés, mushrooms, and a large assortment of cheeses are also characteristic of Limousin. Limousin has a cherry tart, called *clafoutis*, which is the most popular of the many pastries throughout the region. Like Auvergne, Limousin offers little in the way of wine.

The cooking of the Bourbonnais region is very fine. Ancient recipes, like that for *picanchagne*, a pear cake, are jealously guarded. Sheeps' tongues with turnips, *civet d'oie*, meat pies—all are prepared better here than anywhere else. The candies made in Moulins are sold all over France: *palets d'or* (chocolate spangled with gold), *praline rosé* (pink praline), barley sugar, and chocolate truffles. It's fine game country and good also for beef, pork, mutton, poultry, and geese. Some nice light wines come from the Bourbonnais, but is better known for Vichy mineral water. The Bourbonnais region also has its cheeses. Chamberat and Bessay, made from cows' milk, are best known locally, but a small goats' milk cheese called Chevrotin is enjoyed by all French gourmets.

From the mountainous areas of Auvergne and Limousin to the hills and valleys of Bourbonnais, the Massif Central region has excellent raw produce, contributing to its great variety of delicious foods.

Game Salad

SALADE DE PERDREAUX

Serves 4

2 roast partridges, cold, or
   1 3-lb. roast chicken, cold
1 shallot, peeled and chopped
6 tbs. olive oil or,
   ideally, walnut oil
1 tb. tarragon vinegar
1 tsp. prepared mustard
6 small mushrooms
juice of 1 lemon
6 anchovy fillets in oil
6 pickled gherkins
1 tb. capers, drained
1 lettuce heart
few sprigs fresh tarragon (optional)
2 tbs. minced parsley

After you've roasted the game or fowl, this salad is made in a few minutes. It makes a fine lunch.

Carve the birds, discarding the skin and bones. Cut the flesh into fairly large pieces.

In a salad bowl mix the shallot, oil, tarragon vinegar, mustard, salt, and pepper. Add the meat and stir well, lightly coating the game with the dressing. Wipe the mushrooms with a damp towel, trim the stems, and add to the salad bowl. Sprinkle with lemon juice. Cut the anchovy fillets into pieces, and slice the gherkins into chips. Add these and the capers to the salad. Wash and dry the lettuce—use only the freshest leaves in the center. Place these leaves in a circle on a flat dish. Spoon the salad into the center. Sprinkle with the tarragon and parsley.

Bacon and Vegetable Soup

POTÉE

Serves 4

1 cabbage
½ lb. unsliced Canadian bacon
1 pig's foot
4 beef or pork breakfast sausages
3 qts. water
1 large onion, peeled
1 celery stalk, diced
4 large potatoes, peeled
¼ cup butter
8 slices rye bread

This is a hearty peasant soup that is a meal in itself.

Remove the outer leaves and the stem from the cabbage. Slice it in half and put it into a large saucepan with the bacon, pig's foot, and the sausages. Cover with water. Add the onion and the celery to the pan, with a seasoning of salt and pepper. Cook uncovered over high heat for 30 minutes. Then lower the heat, cover, and simmer for 2 hours. After this time, discard the pig's foot and add the potatoes. Cook uncovered for an additional 20 minutes, or until the potatoes are tender. Remove the pan from the heat and lift out the potatoes and the cabbage. Drain both well.

Melt the butter in a skillet. Chop the cabbage and sauté it in the butter along with the potatoes, for a few minutes. Place the sliced bread in the bottom of a heated soup tureen. Strain the stock and pour it over the bread. Place the cabbage and potatoes on a hot serving dish. Then slice the bacon and place it on top, along with the sausages, moistened with a bit of the stock. Serve the soup first, then the meats and vegetables.

Salmon with Sorrel Sauce

SAUMON À L'OSEILLE

Serves 4

4 salmon steaks
¼ cup butter

FOR THE FISH STOCK:
3 mushrooms
few sprigs parsley
1 large onion, peeled and coarsely
    chopped (about 1 scant cup)
1 lb. fish bones, heads, and skin
2 cups water
¼ cup dry white wine
juice of ½ lemon
few peppercorns

FOR THE SAUCE:
2 shallots, peeled and chopped
⅔ cup dry white wine
5 tbs. dry vermouth
3 tbs. heavy cream
2 lbs. fresh sorrel or spinach
½ cup butter
juice of ½ lemon

The pure water of the river Allier, which flows through Auvergne, is a favorite place for salmon. This recipe comes from the freres Troisgros, the famous restaurant keepers of Roanne.

First prepare the fish stock, or fumet. Trim the mushrooms, wipe them with a damp paper towel, and chop. Place them along with parsley and onion in a large saucepan. Add the fish bones, heads, and skin, water, wine, lemon juice, and peppercorns. Season with salt. Boil quickly for 5 minutes. Then cover and simmer gently for 20 minutes. Strain, and the fumet is ready for use.

To make the sauce, place the shallots in a saucepan with the fumet, wine, and vermouth. Bring to a boil and cook over high heat for a few minutes. Lower the heat and simmer, uncovered, until the liquid is reduced by half. Add the cream and reduce further. Finely chop the sorrel or spinach and add it to the saucepan. Bring back to a boil and remove the pan from the heat.

Cut the butter into small pieces and gradually add it to the sauce, beating constantly. Season with salt and pepper and add the lemon juice. Melt the ¼ cup butter in a skillet and add the salmon steaks. Saute over high heat for 2 to 3 minutes on each side.

Pour the sauce onto a heated serving dish, arrange the salmon steaks on top, and serve immediately.

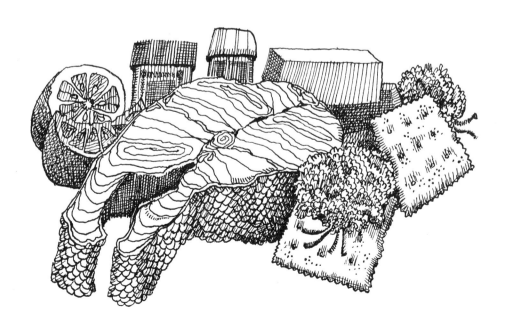

The name of this dish comes from the pot in which it is cooked. A cassette is an earthenware vessel with high sides and no lid. As an alternative, a casserole may be used.

Ask the butcher to cut the knuckle off the leg, or fold it back so that the meat can be placed in the casserole.

Preheat the oven to 400.

Make a deep incision in the lamb near the knuckle, and slide in the garlic cloves. (Peel them or not, according to whether you want a strong or mild garlic taste.) Cube a small piece of the bacon and slice the remainder thinly. Then make six other incisions all over the leg and insert the bacon cubes.

Butter a heavy casserole and lay the potato slices on the bottom along with the sliced bacon. Pour in the water. Add a seasoning of salt and pepper and the bay leaf. Place the lamb on top of the potatoes. Sprinkle with the parsley and thyme. Dot with butter. Place in preheated oven for about 1 hour. For medium-rare lamb, your meat thermometer should read 150. The water should be completely absorbed by the potatoes, and the lamb and the potatoes should be golden brown.

The soufflé is one of the triumphs and glories of French cookery. This carrot soufflé is a delicious, colorful, and unexpected accompaniment for simple roasts and poultry.

Preheat the oven to 375.

Place the carrots and onion in a saucepan with sugar, nutmeg, a pinch of salt, and cold water to cover. Cook gently uncovered for 20 minutes or until the vegetables are tender. Remove the cloves from the onion. Blend the vegetables to a puree, using a food mill or an electric blender. Pour the mixture into a bowl and stir in the cornstarch and the egg yolks. Beat the whites with a dash of salt until they are stiff. Then fold them gently into the puree. Pour the mixture into a well-buttered 6–cup soufflé dish. Set in preheated oven for 25 minutes. The center of the soufflé should be quite soft. Serve immediately.

Leg of Lamb Casserole

GIGOT À LA CASSETTE

Serves 6

1 3½–4-lb. leg of lamb
4 cloves garlic
6 oz. smoked bacon
¼ cup butter
4 large potatoes, peeled and thinly
   sliced (about 8 cups)
1 cup water
1 bay leaf
1 tb. minced parsley
1 tsp. dried thyme
1 tb. butter

> Use three bowls to separate eggs. Crack over the first, letting the white flow into it; put yolk in the second; and, making sure it contains no yolk, transfer the white to the third. Thus only 1 white will be spoiled if you slip.

Carrot Soufflé

SOUFFLÉ DE CAROTTES

Serves 4

8 medium carrots, sliced
1 onion, peeled and stuck with
   4 cloves
1 tsp. sugar
pinch of nutmeg
2 tbs. cornstarch
4 eggs, separated
2 tbs. butter

Boiled Beef

POT-AU-FEU

Serves 6

3 lbs. round steak
3 qts. water
8 leeks
5–6 young turnips
6 small carrots
1 large onion stuck with 4 cloves
2 bay leaves
½ teaspoon dried thyme
few sprigs parsley
1 celery stalk
a few peppercorns
4 large potatoes

> If you peel potatoes in advance, soak them in cold water to avoid discoloration. Dry the potatoes before cooking.

This dish is extremely good, provided it is carefully prepared with top-quality ingredients. Whatever stock is left over can be used as a base for other soups or for making sauces.

Trim the round steak, removing all the fat and leaving the meat in one piece. Bring the water to a boil in a large kettle. Trim, clean, and wash the leeks. Leave them whole. Peel the turnips and carrots and cut them into large chunks. Add the onion and the prepared vegetables to the pot, along with the herbs, celery, salt, and peppercorns. Cook over high heat for 15 minutes. Then add the meat. As soon as the water returns to a boil, lower the heat so the liquid is barely simmering. After 10 minutes or so, skim the surface, partially cover the pot, and cook gently for 2 hours.

Peel the potatoes and add them to the pot after the 2 hours. Cook for an additional 20 minutes. Strain the stock, discard the onions, taste for seasoning, and serve it separately in large cups. Slice the meat and surround it with the vegetables on a serving platter. Accompany with different kinds of mustard, gherkins, and pickles.

Fried Potatoes

TRUFFADE

Serves 4

¼ cup lard
1 shallot, peeled and chopped
¼ tsp. dried thyme
7 slices bacon, diced
2 large potatoes, peeled and thinly sliced (about 4 cups)
1⅓ cups tomme d'Auvergne cheese, or 1 cup cottage cheese plus ⅓ cup grated Swiss cheese

There are no truffles in la truffade; truffle was the name used in the last century for potatoes.

Melt the lard in a skillet and add the shallot. Sprinkle with the thyme. As soon as the shallot is golden, add the diced bacon, and continue to cook, stirring frequently, until the bacon is lightly colored. Dry the potato slices and add them to the pan. Cook over high heat, turning occasionally. Season with salt and pepper. When the potatoes are tender and have slightly golden edges, break up the cheese with a fork and add it to the pan. Cook over moderate heat until the cheese has melted. Serve, surrounded with lettuce, on a heated dish.

Wild Boar in Red Wine

SANGLIER À L'AUVERGNAT

Serves 4

2 lbs. wild boar, or fresh ham or
    picnic shoulder
12 dried juniper berries
1 bottle red wine
1 onion, peeled and stuck with
    4 cloves
1 clove garlic, peeled
few sprigs parsley
3 bay leaves
¼ tsp. dried thyme
grated rind of ½ lemon
2 tbs. butter
5 tbs. oil
4 shallots, peeled and chopped
1 tsp. sugar
⅓ cup Cognac
1 slice rye bread
1 tb. vinegar

There are still a good many wild boar in the forests of Auvergne. This is a classic way of cooking it. You can also use this recipe for a simple pork roast. A puree of chestnuts, potatoes, or lentils usually accompanies this dish.

If you use tender young wild boar, it is not necessary to marinate it the day before: one hour is enough. For older boar (and pork) allow 12 to 14 hours for the marinating.

Roll the meat into a roast, tie it together if necessary, and rub it with 3 crushed juniper berries. For the marinade, place the wine, onion, garlic, parsley, bay leaves, thyme, lemon rind, salt and pepper in a large enameled or glass bowl. Add the meat.

Remove the meat from the marinade and dry it with paper towels. Heat the butter and oil in a large skillet. Add the shallots to the pan and then the meat. Saute gently, turning several times. As soon as the meat is slightly golden, pour over the unstrained marinade. Add the sugar and remaining juniper berries. Cover and cook very gently for 3 hours. Remove the cooked meat from the skillet and strain the liquid into a bowl. Replace the meat in the skillet and pour the (warmed) Cognac over it. Off heat, ignite the Cognac with a match, making certain to turn your face away. When the flames have died, add the strained liquid and cook for an additional 10 minutes.

Trim the crust from the rye bread and cut the bread into small pieces; sprinkle them with vinegar and add to the skillet. Stir and cook for a minute. Serve the meat coated with a little of the sauce, passing the remainder separately.

garlic press

This is a pleasant first course, or a dish which can be made quickly as a light supper.

Beat the eggs, adding half the cream, a little salt and pepper, and the parsley and tarragon. Let the mixture stand while continuing.

Dry the potatoes. Melt the butter in a large skillet and sauté the shallot and diced potatoes. When they are golden, add the diced ham and cook gently, covered, for about 10 minutes, shaking the pan from time to time. Pour in the prepared eggs. Cook over high heat for a few minutes, shaking the pan often. The mixture should be dry on the outside and soft, or just cooked, inside. Remove the skillet from the heat and pour the rest of the cream over the omelet. Flip the omelet onto a heated serving dish, folding it in half, and sprinkle with the grated cheese. Serve immediately.

Potato and Ham Omelet

OMELETTE BRAYAUDE

Serves 4

6 eggs
½ cup heavy cream
1 tb. minced parsley
1 tb. chopped fresh, or
    ½ tsp. dried tarragon
2 medium potatoes, peeled and
    diced (about 2 cups)
¼ cup butter
1 shallot, peeled and finely
    chopped
½ lb. raw or smoked ham or
    lean bacon, diced
¼ cup grated Swiss or
    parmesan cheese

This excellent dessert from Auvergne is similar to the clafoutis of Limousin, which is much better known, but this recipe is made without milk. Traditionally, the stems, but not the pits, of the cherries are removed.

Preheat the oven to 400.

Grease a 12-inch round cake pan or a 9-by-13 loaf pan, using a third of the butter, and place half the cherries in the bottom. Put the sifted flour in a bowl and make a well in the center. Add the eggs, sugar, water, and a pinch of salt. Stir, drawing the mixture together, then beat to a smooth batter. Pour the batter into the pan, spread it evenly, and cover with the rest of the cherries. Dot the surface with the remaining butter. Bake for about 30 minutes in the preheated oven. Allow the cake to cool before removing it from the pan.

Cherry Pudding

MILLIARD

Serves 4

7 tbs. butter
1 lb. Bing cherries
2¾ cups sifted all-purpose flour
3 eggs
¼ cup sugar
½ cup water

Provence

Provence is in many ways the most appealing area in France. It borders the beautiful Mediterranean Sea, and within it is the glamorous French Riviera and such intriguing cities as Marseilles, Cannes, St. Tropez, Nice, and Aix-en-Provence.

The climate is warm, and clouds are a rarity. The sun shines almost all year round, giving a luminosity to colors. It is perhaps this brightness of color that has traditionally attracted painters to the region: Cezanne was born in Provence, and others such as Van Gogh, Renoir, Matisse, and Picasso did much of their work in the region.

Provence is the country of the olive: small and large, dry and juicy, hard and soft; white, purple, black, green. The olive is an integral ingredient in almost every dish in this region. Garlic and tomatoes are used throughout France, but nowhere more so than in Provence. Just about any dish on a menu listed as *à la provençale* contains cooked tomatoes and garlic.

Most local recipes are based on the produce of the sea and the mountains: mutton, game (such as wild boar and rabbit, snipe, plover, and wild fowl), cheese made from ewes' and goats' milk, and honey. Many dishes are flavored with the wild herbs that grow on the slopes of the sun-drenched hills. Some famous specialties of the region are the *bouillabaisse* of Marseilles, *ratatouille*, *aïoli* (a delicious garlic-flavored mayonnaise often served with raw vegetables), fish, and *soupe à l'ail* (garlic soup). Egg dishes are popular—for example, poached eggs on half tomatoes in tomato-and-garlic sauce with eggplant; omelets made with diced tomatoes and garlic.

In Nice and Antibes, different types of nourishing pasta are made by the local housewives and innkeepers. These are best eaten fresh. Marseilles is renowned for its *pieds et paquets*, sheep tripe filled with salt pork, flavored with herbs, and cooked in white wine and tomato sauce. In the mountains, truffles—fleshy, potato-shaped fungi, similar to mushrooms, which grow underground—are found by specially trained pigs or dogs, who dig them up from beneath the oak trees. Vegatables are abundant and profusely used. They are selected and cooked carefully, frequently in combination with onions, oil, and herbs. Green vegetables are cooked quickly to retain their full flavor and color. The best method is to plunge them into a large pot of rapidly boiling water and quickly remove them just as soon as they are done. Stuffed vegetables are a favorite first course and are served either hot or cold. The most popular vegetable is the tomato, followed by onions, eggplant, summer squash, cardoons, fennel, peppers, and superb artichokes.

Many of the desserts in this region are made with marzipan, for there are many almond trees, but the hot, dry climate is not conducive to elaborate pastries and desserts. On the other hand, candied fruits and flowers are quite popular. Orange, lemon, tangerine, grapefruit, fig, and even banana trees grow on the Côte d'Azur. Tasty melons are cultivated inland, and some are crystallized. Other, more common fruit trees—peach, quince, apricot, and cherry—blossom in the spring.

The most famous wines are those of the Rhone valley, Châteauneuf-du-Pape and Côte Rotie. Some of the lesser known wines from the coast of Provence also delight the gourmet: The white Cassis, the rosé of Bandol, and the light wine of the Camarque are perfect accompaniments to a Provençal meal. There are few spirits distilled in this region, but one must mention the eau-de-vie of Cassis and of Roquevaire, and the liqueurs perfumed with herbs—such as those of Larins and Saint-Michel-de-Frigolet—which are made by the monks from old, secret recipes.

Justifiably famous for its substantial wines, the vineyards of Provence produce over twenty million gallons each year. Although most is classified *ordinaire*, much of it is popular in Europe and the United States. Unlike some French wines, these travel well and so are exported widely.

Herbs are found in the most of the dishes in Provence, as well as in the liqueurs: garlic, thyme, rosemary, basil, fennel, wild thyme, and even lavender (a single leaf in a sauce can make a dish fit for the gods). The other factor common to all the cooking of the region is the fragrant greenish-golden oil, pressed from locally grown olives, which is the basic cooking fat. Perhaps this is the secret of the good health and gaiety of the people of Provence. It is understandable that the visitor from a cold, noisy city may wish to linger in the golden light and enjoy the special feeling of well-being that surrounds him here.

Mixed Vegetable Stew

RATATOUILLE

Serves 6

2 large eggplants
4–6 small zucchini
1 tb. coarse (kosher) salt
3 sweet peppers, red and green, if
    possible
⅓ cup olive oil
2 medium onions, peeled and
    sliced (about 1½ cups)
2 cloves garlic, peeled and
    chopped
4 tbs. minced parsley
1 tsp. dried thyme
1 bay leaf
6–8 medium tomatoes, peeled,
    seeded, and chopped

This dish, which originated in Provence, is now cooked throughout France. It is equally good hot or cold and can be prepared in advance—some feel it improves with reheating.

Peel the eggplants and cut into pieces about 2 inches long and ½ inch wide. Scrub the zucchini, but do not peel. Slice as you did the eggplant. Place the two vegetables in a colander or bowl and toss with the salt. Let stand for half an hour. Drain and dry the slices. Trim the sweet peppers, removing the stems and seeds, and chop the flesh.

Heat the oil in a large heavy saucepan and sauté the onions, garlic, and parsley. Add the thyme, bay leaf, eggplant, zucchini, and tomatoes. Season with salt and pepper. Cook uncovered over high heat for 5 minutes. Then cover and lower the heat. Cook for an additional 20 minutes, stirring from time to time and, if necessary, adding enough water to keep the mixture moist.

Sautéed Potatoes

POMMES DE TERRE
AUX ANCHOIS

Serves 4

8 medium potatoes
3 cloves garlic (or to taste)
⅓ cup olive oil
2 tbs. minced parsley
sprig chopped fresh, or
    ¼ tsp. dried basil (optional)
8 anchovy fillets in oil
juice of 1 lemon

This recipe, especially popular in the mountains of Provence, is an excellent first course.

Cook the potatoes in lightly salted boiling water for about 12 minutes or until they are barely tender. Drain and cool for a few moments. Then cut the potatoes into thick slices. You should have about 8 cups. Peel the garlic cloves. Heat the oil in a skillet; add 1 clove of garlic. As soon as the garlic begins to sizzle, add the potatoes, and fry until they are golden brown, turning frequently. Chop the rest of the garlic finely and combine with the parsley and basil. Remove the potatoes from the skillet and place on a heated serving dish. Cut the anchovies into small pieces. Add them to the potatoes and sprinkle with the garlic, parsley, basil, and lemon juice.

Bouillabaisse

BOUILLABAISSE

Serves 6

2 medium onions, peeled and
    chopped (about 2 cups)

2 leeks, cleaned and coarsely
    chopped

3 medium tomatoes, peeled and
    seeded

4 cloves garlic, crushed

1 tb. chopped parsley

½ tsp. fennel seed

5 tbs. olive oil

6 cups water

2 cups dry white wine

1 bay leaf

1 tsp. saffron

6 lbs. fresh fish, from among the
    following, as available: sea bass,
    red snapper, haddock, cod,
    rockfish, eel, halibut, hake

1 medium lobster, or 12 jumbo
    shrimp (optional)

1 qt. mussels (optional)

12 slices French bread

Bouillabaisse, a Mediterranean fisherman's soup, is flavored with the herbs and spices of the region. Ideally, you should choose a variety of fish, combining those that are firm-fleshed with others that are flaky and tender. Shellfish are not traditional, but they add color and flavor if you wish to include them.

Mix the onions, leeks, tomatoes, garlic, parsley, and fennel seed in a bowl. Heat the olive oil in a large kettle and add the prepared mixture. Sauté for about 3 minutes, stirring. Then add the water, white wine, bay leaf, saffron, a large pinch of salt, and pepper. Simmer for 10 minutes.

In the meantime, wash and clean the fish. Separate the large firm-fleshed fish (bass, halibut, eel) from the small tender fish (cod, hake). Cut the large fish into chunks; leave the small ones whole. Add the chunks of firm-fleshed fish to the kettle, along with the optional lobster or shrimp. Simmer gently for 7 minutes. If you are using them, scrub and wash the mussels under cold running water. Add them to the kettle along with the rest of the fish. Cook for an additional 3 minutes, or until the mussels open. Heat a large soup tureen under hot water and quickly wipe it dry. Fill the tureen with bread slices and pour in the contents of the kettle. Serve immediately.

Garlic is an essential flavoring in the cooking of Provence. Paradoxically, it is the way the garlic is cooked rather than the amount that generally determines the strength of its taste. When the cloves are cooked whole and unbruised, their final flavor is subtle. To peel, drop into a pan of boiling water for 1 minute, drain, and run under cold water. Carefully slip off the skins.

Chicken Provençal Style

POULET SAUTÉ À LA PROVENÇALE

Serves 4

1 3½-lb. chicken
6 tbs. olive oil
1½ tbs. butter
1 cup dry white wine
2 cloves garlic, peeled
white pepper
1 tsp. sugar
4 large or 6 small tomatoes, peeled,
    seeded, juiced, and chopped
4 anchovy fillets in oil
1 tb. chopped fresh, or
    ½ tsp. dried basil
16 pitted black olives
8 pitted green olives

This is a delicious way of preparing chicken. The olives, anchovies, garlic, tomatoes, oil, and wine are typical ingredients of this region.

Cut the chicken into 8 pieces and dry the pieces. Reserve the giblets and liver for another dish. Heat the oil with the butter in a large heavy saucepan and brown the chicken pieces. Add the white wine and bring to a boil. Turn the heat very low. Add the garlic, pepper, sugar, and tomatoes. Cook for 30 minutes. Cut the anchovy fillets into small pieces (it is because they are salty that no additional salt is required). Add the anchovies and basil with the olives (green olives are not traditional but give more flavor). Cook over moderate heat for a further 20 minutes and serve.

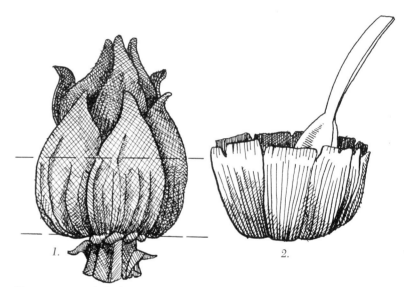

To prepare artichoke hearts, remove the outside leaves. Cut off the stem close to the base and slice remaining cone of leaves above the choke (1). After simmering, remove the choke with a spoon and trim. (2).

Like carpe à la camarguaise, this recipe comes from Oustàu de Baumanière *at Les Baux.*

Artichoke Mousse

MOUSSELINE D'ARTICHAUTS

Serves 4

8 medium artichokes
3 tbs. heavy cream
¼ cup butter

For the puree, you should use only the hearts of the artichokes. You need not throw away the rest. Keep the tender leaves and boil them in water. Use the strained stock for soups.

Cover the artichoke hearts with boiling water and simmer, covered, for about 35 minutes. Drain, remove choke, and press through a sieve to make a puree. Beat in the cream, butter, and seasoning. As an alternative, blend the hearts to a smooth puree in an electric blender. Then add the cream and butter and blend to a smooth mousse. Just before serving, reheat in a bain-marie.

This salad is popular throughout France. It is frequently served as a first course for a summer meal or as a luncheon entrée.

Place the drained and quartered tomatoes in a salad bowl. Slice the pepper into thin strips and broil it quickly (or dry-fry in a nonstick skillet)—this is done to heighten the flavor. Break the tuna fish into big pieces. Cut the anchovy fillets in half. Wash and peel the radishes, leaving on the small tops. Add the tuna, anchovy fillets, radishes, and olives to the tomatoes in the salad bowl. Mix the oil, vinegar, mustard, and pepper in a small jar. Shake vigorously and pour the dressing over the salad. Serve immediately.

Salad Niçoise

SALADE NIÇOISE

Serves 4

8 small or 6 large tomatoes, peeled
   and quartered
1 green pepper, trimmed and
   seeded
6½–7 oz. can tuna fish in oil,
   drained
anchovy fillets in oil
12 pink radishes (optional)
20 pitted ripe olives
⅓ cup olive oil
2 tbs. wine vinegar
1 tsp. prepared mustard

This recipe is another provided by Monsieur Thuilier, the owner of Oustàu de Baumanière.

Preheat the oven to 300.

Wash the carp under cold running water and dry carefully. Place the fish in a shallow greased baking dish. Sprinkle with olive oil, season with salt and pepper, and add the herbs. Put the dish in the oven and bake for 45 minutes. As soon as it begins to turn brown or becomes crisp (after about 20 or 30 minutes), pour in the white wine and add the tomatoes and mushrooms. Continue to cook very slowly for an additional 15 to 20 minutes.

When ready to serve, place the carp on a heated serving dish and pour the liquid in which it has cooked into a small saucepan. Blend the cornstarch with the butter to make beurre manié and over low heat add it in pieces to the saucepan. Stir constantly until the sauce is well blended and thickened. Pour the sauce over the carp and serve.

Baked Carp

CARPE À LA CAMARGUAISE

Serves 4

1 carp, about 2 lbs., skinned and
   cleaned
¾ cup olive oil
2–3 tbs., combined, of fresh herbs
   such as thyme, savory, fennel,
   basil; or 1 tb. of these
   herbs dried
½ bottle dry white wine
3 tomatoes, peeled, seeded, juiced
   and chopped
3 large mushrooms, sliced thinly
2 tbs. cornstarch
2 tbs. butter

Baked Red Mullet

ROUGETS AU VIN BLANC

Serves 4

1 2–3 lb. red mullet
3 tbs. butter
½ tsp. dried thyme
1 large onion, peeled and chopped
   (about 1 scant cup)
1 clove garlic, peeled and chopped
2 tbs. minced parsley
¾ cup white wine

Red mullet, widely available in the southern United States, is one of the very few fish which connoisseurs prefer not cleaned.

Preheat the oven to 400.

Wash and dry the fish and place it on a well greased oven-proof dish. Dot with butter, and sprinkle with thyme, season with salt and pepper. Scatter the onion, garlic, and parsley over the fish. Pour in ½ the white wine and bake for 30 to 40 minutes. Baste the fish from time to time with the hot wine in the dish, adding more wine as necessary.

❧

Cheese Dumplings

GNOCCHI GRATINÉS AU FROMAGE

Serves 6

8 medium potatoes
¼ cup butter, softened
2 eggs, beaten
pinch of nutmeg
2 tbs. minced parsley
½ cup plus 4 tablespoons grated
   Swiss cheese
about 1 cup all-purpose flour
4 large tomatoes, peeled, seeded,
   and juiced
1 tsp. oregano

This is an inexpensive and delicious recipe that may be served as a main course at a light meal.

Cook the potatoes uncovered in boiling water until they are tender, about 20 minutes. Drain and mash them. Mix the potatoes in a bowl with the butter, beaten eggs, nutmeg, parsley, 4 tablespoons of the Swiss cheese, salt, and pepper until the ingredients are well blended.

In a large saucepan or kettle, bring several quarts of salted water to a boil.

Spread the flour on a plate. Shape the potato mixture into small balls about the size of walnuts and roll them in the flour, coating each generously. Add the gnocchi, a few at a time, to the boiling water. When they rise to the surface they are done. Remove the gnocchi from the pan with a slotted spoon and arrange them on a well greased oven-proof dish.

Chop the tomatoes and spread them over the gnocchi. Sprinkle with the rest of the grated cheese and the oregano. Bake for about 15 minutes, then run quickly under the broiler to brown.

Lamb Stew

SAUTÉ D'AGNEAU À LA MODE
DES ALPILLES

Serves 4

2 lbs. boned shoulder of lamb,
    cubed
½ cup olive oil
2 tbs. butter
4 shallots, peeled and chopped
2 tbs. minced parsley
1 tsp. oregano
4–6 large tomatoes, peeled,
    seeded, and juiced
½ cup pitted green olives
1 cup rosé wine
1 tsp. sugar
½ lb. small mushrooms

Shallots, are small, delicately flavored members of the onion family. If this aromatic vegetable is unavailable you may substitute the minced white part of a scallion.

This is a pleasant dish to eat in spring. It is often served with pasta.

Dry the cubes of lamb with paper towels. Heat the oil and butter in a large heavy skillet or sauté pan. Add the lamb, shallots, and parsley to the pan. Sprinkle with the oregano and season with salt and pepper. Sauté for a few moments, shaking the pan from time to time. Add the halved tomatoes to the pan, along with the olives, and sauté over high heat for a minute or two. Pour in the wine. Add the sugar and cook for 1 hour over low heat stirring from time to time. Wipe the mushrooms with a damp cloth and add them to the pan. Cook for an additional 5 minutes and serve.

To peel a tomato, drop it into boiling water to cover for 10 seconds. Remove, cut out the stem, and peel. The blanching loosens the skin and it peels off easily. To seed and juice, cut the tomato in half crosswise and gently squeeze each half. If the juice is to be used, squeeze over a strainer placed on a bowl or measuring cup.

Garlic Mayonnaise

A ÏOLI

Makes 1 to 11/2 cups

2 small heads of garlic
2 egg yolks
1 cup olive oil
juice of 1 lemon
1 tsp. cold water

Aïoli is served as an appetizer with raw vegetables, cold meats or fish, and hard-boiled eggs.

Peel the garlic and pound it in a mortar. Add the egg yolks and mix slowly. Add a pinch of salt. Then, beating constantly with a whisk, begin to incorporate the olive oil, drop by drop, as for mayonnaise. When the sauce thickens, after you have used about half the oil, you can add the oil by teaspoonfuls. Finish by mixing in the lemon juice and water.

Although it loses somewhat in texture, this recipe can be prepared in an electric blender. Place the peeled and roughly chopped garlic in the container of the blender, along with the egg yolks, salt, and lemon juice. Cover and blend at low speed for a few moments. Remove the center cap in the lid and slowly pour in the oil. When the mixture has thickened and all the oil is added, add the water.

Tomatoes, cheese, and herbs combine to make this pleasant first course.

Preheat the oven to 400.

Slice the top off each tomato and with a small spoon remove the seeds. Mix together the herbs, garlic, and cheese. Beat the eggs and stir them in. Season generously with salt and pepper and fill the hollowed-out tomatoes with the mixture. Arrange the tomatoes in a well-greased ovenproof baking dish and bake in the preheated oven for 12 minutes.

❧

This recipe makes a delicious dessert, especially in summer or after a heavy meal.

To make the pastry, measure the flour into a bowl. Cut the butter into pieces and add it to the flour. Rub lightly between your fingers, allowing the mixture to fall back into the bowl. When the butter is evenly distributed and the mixture is in small, uneven pieces, add water and a pinch of salt. Mix to a rough dough. Then shape the dough into a ball and pass it from one hand to another for 1 minute, without kneading. It will become soft. Cover with a cloth and place it in the refrigerator.

Peel the lemons, removing as much of the pith as possible, and cut the flesh into slices, removing the seeds. Put the lemon slices into a saucepan with the sugar and water. Bring to a boil and cook gently for about 15 minutes, stirring all the time. Remove the pan from the heat and cool.

Preheat the oven to 400.

Roll the pastry into a circle on a floured board. Thoroughly grease an 8-inch pie plate and line it with the dough. Lightly beat one egg and use half to brush the edges of the pastry. For the filling, add the other half of the beaten egg to the remaining whole egg and beat slightly with a fork. Mix into the lemon mixture. Pour the filling into the pastry case and bake in the preheated oven for about 20 minutes. The pie is done when the edges of the pastry come away from the sides of the pie plate. Serve warm, if possible.

Stuffed Tomatoes

TOMATES VALDEBLORE

Serves 4

8 medium tomatoes
few sprigs chopped fresh, or
    1 tsp. dried tarragon
1 tb. minced parsley
2 cloves garlic, crushed
1 cup grated Swiss cheese
2 eggs

Lemon Pie

TARTE AU CITRON À LA
MENTONNAISE

Serves 6

FOR THE PASTRY:
1¼ cups sifted all-purpose flour
⅓ cup butter
¼ cup water
1 egg

FOR THE FILLING:
3 large or 4 small lemons
1¼ cups sugar
⅓ cup water
1 egg

Burgundy and Lyonnais

The names "Burgundy" and "Beaune" immediately conjure up visions of vineyards and glorious wines. Connoisseurs can trace and purchase Burgundy's vintage wines from as far back as the 1860s for red wine and the 1890s for white. This is possible because Burgundy, with its low sloping hills that catch the early morning sunlight, has the greatest vineyard growths in France, with Bordeaux being the only close competitor. The wines are robust and have wonderful bouquet and power. While they may take longer to make, Burgundy's wines are able to live many years.

Northern Burgundy is the home of the famous Chablis wine; from farther south come the most distinguished wines of the Côte de Nuits and Côte de Beaune. Beaune is famous also for the annual wine auction, held in its miraculously preserved medieval almshouse. Once a year, restaurant-owners and connoisseurs come from all over the world to bid for these noble wines.

Burgundy is so highly renowned for good food that many gourmets compare it favorably to the Ile-de-France region. Burgundian cooking is *cuisine bourgeoise* raised to the highest pinnacle. Home cooking is superb, and the delicious specialties include ham with parsley jelly (for Easter Sunday), suckling pig in aspic, and the subtly flavored *oeufs en meurette* (eggs poached in red wine).

Mustard, beef, and wine have a particular influence on Burgundy cooking. Mustard plants grow profusely in Dijon, which makes about half of all the mustard made in France. The quality and variety of Dijon mustards are recognized by gourmets all over the world.

Because of the highly superior breed of cattle raised here, Burgundy beef dishes are extremely popular throughout France. The charolais white steer, a rather new breed, is generally considered the quality-beef animal of all France. *Boeuf à la bourguignonne*, a particularly well-known dish, is Burgundy beef cooked in a red wine sauce and served with mushrooms, small onions, and tiny pieces of bacon. Next to beef, *escargots* (snails) is the most famous Burgundian dish, and Burgundy's *escargots* are said to be the best in France.

Many of the foods of Burgundy are prepared with cream sauces (not surprisingly, considering the abundance of cows in this region). Plain or highly seasoned cream sauces are often served with fish, fowl, mushrooms, and ham.

In northern Burgundy excellent pike and crayfish dishes are prepared, as well as the delicious *gougère* (an unsweetened cheesecake), and succulent cherries. Continuing south, one finds pig, ham, freshwater fish, excellent vegetables, honey, *feuilleté aux morilles* (a nonsweet pastry), gingerbread, and *pralines* (almonds coated with sugar).

Black currants, one of many mouth-watering fruits, is distilled into Cassis liqueur. There is even a "national" aperitif, Kir, a mixture of white wine and black-currant syrup which is named after Canon Kir, for many years deputy-mayor of Dijon.

In ancient times, Lyons was the capital of Gaul. Reunited with France in the reign of Philippe-le-Bel, it is now the third most important city in the country, with half a million people (three million live in Paris). The people of Lyons are probably the most exacting gourmets in France. Less gay and expansive than the Burgundians, they love dark, out-of-the-way restaurants, where one may sample *andouillettes* (tripe sausages), or pigs' feet, washed down with Beaujolais or a good bottle of Côtes du Rhone.

Several of the recipes of Lyons have a quality which can be traced to the early Germanic heritage of the people. A favorite and perhaps one of the most famous of all Lyonnaise dishes is the *quenelle*, derived from the German *knödel* or dumpling. The *quenelles* of Lyons are prepared by dedicated chefs who pride themselves on the lengthy task involved to produce these soufflélike delicacies.

Many dishes are flavored with onion, such as *omelette à la lyonnaise* (an omelet filled with onions and parsley), *pommes de terre lyonnaises*, (fried potatoes cooked with onion), *gras double à la lyonnaise* (tripe cooked with onions and parsley), and a special casserole of veal liver with onion. Sausage and chicken specialties also come from Lyons, as does the well-known cheese Mont d'Or.

The cooking of Lyons has a reputation for excellence and, indeed, many of the cooks of Europe and America have used Lyonnaise techniques as a basis for their fame. The great recipes of a region can rarely be exactly duplicated outside the area because all great regional cooking is based on native products. However, Lyons offers a wide and succulent choice of recipes to those who are not fortunate enough to live there.

Parslied Ham in Aspic

JAMBON PERSILLÉ

Serves 12

1 4-lb. raw smoked picnic ham

FOR THE JELLY:
4 shallots, peeled
2 calf's feet
1 lb. veal knuckle
bouquet garni
1 clove garlic, peeled
4¾ cups dry white wine
2 tbs. vinegar
2 cups tightly packed minced
   parsley

> The jelly may be made from a gelatin powder base to which wine and parsley are added, as described on the package.

Kidneys in White Wine

ROGNONS AU VIN BLANC

Serves 4

¼ lb. mushrooms
½ cup butter
1 shallot, peeled and chopped
1 clove garlic, crushed
1 tb. minced parsley
4 lamb kidneys
1 tsp. prepared mustard
¾ cup dry white wine
3 white peppercorns, bruised
1 tb. all-purpose flour

This is a very tasty dish for a summer lunch or picnic. It is traditionally served on Easter Sunday.

Soak the ham in cold water for 12 hours, changing the water from time to time. Place it in a large saucepan, cover with cold water, and bring to a boil. Lower the heat and cook gently for an hour. Drain off the liquid and discard it.

In a heavy casserole, place the ham, shallots, calf's feet, veal knuckle, bouquet garni, garlic, a grinding of pepper, and the white wine. Add enough water to cover and put on the lid. Bring to a boil, lower the heat, and simmer gently for 2 hours. Remove the casserole from the heat and let the ham cool in the liquid.

When the ham is cold, remove it from the liquid, strip off the rind, and remove any bone. Chop the ham and place in an earthenware dish, pressing down well.

Strain the liquid from the casserole through a strainer lined with cheesecloth. Then place in the refrigerator for 1 hour. When the jelly is half-set, add the vinegar and parsley. Pour this jelly mixture over the minced ham. Cover with foil and return to the refrigerator to allow the jelly to set.

❧

This delicate traditional first course is particularly popular in Burgundy.

Trim the mushrooms, wipe them clean with a damp paper towel, and thinly slice them lengthwise. Heat 2 tablespoons of the butter in a small saucepan. Add the shallot, garlic, parsley, and mushrooms. Sauté for 1 or 2 minutes over high heat. Cover the pan, lower the heat, and cook for 5 minutes. Remove the pan from the heat.

Peel off the fine filament and cut off the fat from the underside of the kidneys. Slice the kidneys thinly. Heat the remainder of the butter in a skillet and, when hot, add the kidneys. Cook for 3 minutes, turning occasionally.

Mix the mustard with the white wine and bruised peppercorns. Sprinkle the kidneys with flour, stir, and the whitewine mixture and then the mushroom mixture. Cook for a further 3 minutes over gentle heat to thicken the sauce. Pour the sauce into a heated serving dish.

The kidneys may be served on slices of buttered toast or on bread fried in butter.

Cheese Pastry Ring

GOUGÈRE

Serves 6

1 cup milk
½ cup butter
1 cup sifted all-purpose flour
pinch of nutmeg
3 eggs
¼ lb. Swiss cheese
1 egg, beaten, for glazing

Based on choux pastry, this cheese delicacy may be served as a first course or with cocktails.

Preheat the oven to 400.

Put the milk, butter, and a pinch of salt into a saucepan. Bring slowly to a boil, stirring constantly. When the liquid boils, immediately pour in the flour and stir briskly with a wooden spoon. Continue to cook over low heat for a few minutes, beating well until the mixture has thickened. Remove the pan from the heat and beat for a minute or two. Then add the nutmeg and the whole eggs, one by one, beating constantly after each addition. Cut the Swiss cheese into small, very thin slices and add it to the mixture. Thoroughly grease and flour a flat baking sheet. Spoon the dough onto it in the shape of a ring. Glaze with the beaten egg. Place in the center of the preheated oven and bake for about 20 minutes. Cut the baked gougere in slices and serve hot.

❧

Eggs Poached in Red Wine

OEUFS EN MEURETTE

Serves 4

5 tbs. butter
12 small white onions, peeled
5 slices bacon, diced
2 tbs. minced parsley
2 carrots
1 leek
½ bottle dry red Burgundy
1 tsp. sugar
4 eggs
1 tb. oil
4 slices bread

This is a delicious first course or luncheon dish which should be served with the same Burgundy as was used in the cooking.

Melt 3 tablespoons of the butter in a skillet and saute the onions for 5 to 7 minutes. Add the diced bacon and the parsley. Season moderately with salt and lavishly with pepper. Cook until the onions are golden, stirring frequently.

Meanwhile, peel and thinly slice the carrots. Clean the leek, remove the base and the green top. Finely chop the white part. Add the wine to the pan, a little at a time, stirring constantly. Add the sugar, carrots, and leek. Cook gently for 15 minutes, stirring from time to time. Break the eggs, one by one, into a small cup. Add each egg to the sauce quickly. As soon as they are all added, remove the pan from the heat and leave for 5 minutes—the eggs will poach in the heat of the sauce.

Heat the remaining 2 tablespoons of butter with the oil in a skillet and fry the slices of bread over high heat until they are golden brown. Arrange the bread on a warm serving dish. Lift the eggs gently out of the sauce with a slotted spoon and place one on each slice of bread. Cover with the strained sauce.

This traditional method of cooking turnips is particularly good. Serve turnips with fowl or roasts.

Peel the turnips and cook them whole in boiling salted water for 15 minutes. Drain and sprinkle them lightly with nutmeg and pepper. Melt the butter in a heavy saucepan and sauté the turnips for 1 minute over moderate heat. Sprinkle in the flour, stir, and then add the stock, a little at a time, stirring constantly. Add the parsley and the sugar. Cover and cook gently for 10 minutes.

Just before serving, mix the 2 egg yolks in a bowl and stir in a little of the liquid in which the turnips were cooked. Return this to the saucepan, stirring it slowly into the rest of the liquid. Cook for only a moment or two and remove the pan from the heat. The egg yolks should not boil. Serve the turnips immediately, coated with the sauce, in a serving dish.

Turnips in Egg Sauce

NAVETS À L'ANCIENNE

Serves 4

8–10 small young turnips
pinch of nutmeg
3 tbs. butter
1 tb. all-purpose flour
1 cup beef stock or canned beef
   bouillon
2 tbs. minced parsley
1 tb. sugar
2 egg yolks

Chicken Baked in Crust

POULET EN CROÛTE

Serves 4

1 2–2½ lb. frying chicken

FOR THE STUFFING:
2½ cups bread crumbs, lightly packed
¼ cup milk
1 egg
3 tbs. Cognac
5 slices bacon, diced
2 tbs. minced parsley
¼ tsp. dried thyme

FOR THE PASTRY:
1½ cups sifted all-purpose flour
½ cup butter
4–5 tbs. water
1 egg, beaten, for glazing

Variations of this dish are found in many other regions. This preparation is based on a very old recipe. It is impressive and easy to prepare.

Dry the chicken with paper towels. Soak the bread crumbs in the milk, beaten egg, and Cognac. Season with salt and pepper. Stir in the bacon and herbs. Mix well and stuff the cavity of the chicken. Sew up the opening with strong white thread.

Sift the flour for the pastry into a bowl. Add the butter in pieces and mix quickly with your fingertips. Stir in the water and a pinch of salt. Knead to a dough and shape into a ball. Let rest for 15 minutes. Then place the dough on a floured board and roll it out thinly to a circle large enough to completely cover the chicken.

Preheat the oven to 400.

Place the chicken, on its side, on one half of the pastry, with the breastbone toward the center of the circle. Moisten the edge of the circle. Fold over the second half of the pastry to enclose the chicken. Seal the pastry where it joins, which will be along the backbone of the bird. Turn the bird breast side up and seal the ends.

Place on a greased baking sheet and brush the pastry with beaten egg. Bake in the preheated oven for 30 minutes. Lower the heat to 350, cover with foil, and bake for an additional 30 minutes. To serve, cut away both leg joints. Then carve the chicken, cutting through both pastry and chicken flesh.

1.

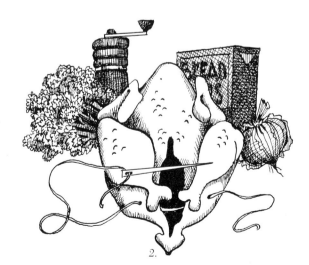

2.

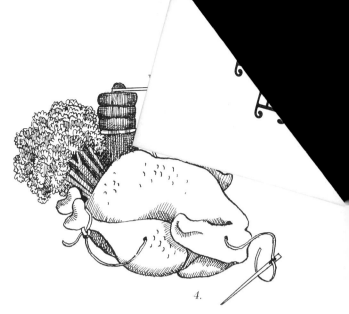

To truss a chicken or other small fowl, insert a trussing or mattress needle threaded with white string through the lower part of the carcass (1). Reinsert the needle over a drumstick and through the other drumstick. Tie the string securely, but do not cut (2). Insert the needle through the thigh and body, emerging at the same position on the other side (3). Turn the fowl on its breast, fold the wings back, and thrust the needle through the wings, catching the neck skin. Pull the string tightly and tie firmly (4).

This is one of the good, simple recipes of the great chef Alexandre Dumaine, who is considered by many authorities to be the greatest chef of our time.

Remove the skin and heads from the fish and separate the flesh into fillets. Place the skin and bones in a saucepan with water to cover. Add a seasoning of salt and pepper, and the bouquet garni. Simmer for 20 minutes. Strain the liquid and reserve it for cooking the fish.

Preheat the oven to 350.

Grease an ovenproof baking dish and arrange the fillets on it. Sprinkle the shallots over them along with a very little salt. Moisten with the wine and the reserved fish stock. Cover with greased foil, the greased side next to the fish fillets. Bake in the preheated oven for 15 minutes. Remove the fish from the liquid and keep it warm while finishing the sauce.

Pour the liquid in which the fish cooked into a saucepan and reduce it by half over high heat. Remove the pan from the heat and, beating constantly with a wire whisk, add the butter by small pieces. Pour the sauce over the sole and serve immediately.

Sole in White Wine

SOLES AU CHABLIS

Serves 4

2 sole, about 1 lb. each
bouquet garni
2 shallots, peeled and finely
    chopped
¾ cup Chablis or
    other dry white wine
3 tbs. butter

Freshwater Fish in Red Wine

PAUCHOUSE

Serves 8

3¼ lbs. freshwater fish such as
  trout, carp, eel, or pike
1 bottle red Burgundy
1 tsp. sugar
1 bay leaf
½ tsp. dried thyme
1 onion, peeled and stuck with
  3 cloves
2 cloves garlic, crushed
2 tbs. minced parsley
⅓ cup Cognac
2 tbs. butter
1 tb. all-purpose flour

Beef Stew in Red Wine

BOEUF BOURGUIGNON

Serves 4

3 lbs. chuck
1 tb. oil
2 tbs. butter
1 shallot, peeled and chopped
½ bottle dry red wine, preferably
  Burgundy
1¼ cups beef stock or
  canned beef bouillon
1 onion, peeled and stuck with
  2 cloves
¼ tsp. dried thyme
2 bay leaves
1 tsp. sugar
¼ lb. small mushrooms
5 slices fat bacon
2 tbs. minced parsley
1 tb. cornstarch
2 tbs. water

This recipe is a specialty of Saint-Jean-Losne. In other parts of Burgundy, it is prepared with white wine.

Clean the fish, remove the heads, and cut the rest into large pieces. Gently heat the wine in a saucepan with the sugar, bay leaf, thyme, onion, garlic, parsley, salt, and pepper. Bring to a boil and immerse the pieces of fish in it. Turn the heat low and cook for 15 minutes. Remove the pieces of fish and arrange them on a hot serving dish. Leave the liquid in the saucepan. Warm the Cognac and pour it over the fish. Averting your face, ignite the Cognac with a match. Shake the pan to spread the flames. When the flames have died, place the dish in a warm oven to keep hot.

Blend the butter and flour together in a bowl and mix with 3 to 4 tablespoons of the cooking liquid. Return to the saucepan, stirring briskly all the time. Cook over high heat, stirring constantly, for 1 to 2 minutes until the sauce has thickened and is boiling. Pour over the fish and serve immediately.

❦

You can prepare this delicious beef dish completely ahead—it gains in flavor when reheated.

Cut the beef into large cubes, remove all the fat, and dry the pieces with paper towels. Heat the oil and butter in a casserole or skillet and add the pieces of meat and the shallot. Sauté until the meat is browned on all sides. Gradually add the wine and the stock. Add the onion, the thyme, and the bay leaves. Stir in the sugar and season with pepper and only a little salt, as the stock is salty. Cover and simmer for 1½ hours over low heat.

Trim the mushrooms and wipe them clean with a damp paper towel. Dice the bacon and sauté it gently in a skillet until it has browned lightly. Add the minced parsley and mushrooms to the bacon and cook for 3 or 4 minutes.

About 10 minutes before the beef has finished cooking, add the parsley, mushrooms, and bacon to the casserole. Moisten the cornstarch with 2 tablespoons water and stir the paste into the casserole. Bring to a boil, stirring briskly. If not to be served immediately, let the stew cool, cover, and refrigerate. Before serving, reheat for about 20 minutes over moderate heat stirring from time to time.

There is no tripe in this dish, and the name of this old recipe remains a mystery. It is a first-course specialty of the region.

Hard-boil the eggs for 12 minutes in simmering water and then place them in a bowl of cold water. Place the onions in a saucepan of boiling water and cook for 10 minutes over high heat; then drain. Shell and slice the eggs.

To prepare the sauce, melt the butter in a saucepan, sprinkle in the flour, and stir briskly over moderate heat. Add the milk, a little at a time, stirring constantly. Season with the nutmeg, salt, and pepper. Cook gently for 5 minutes. Add the parsely and sliced eggs along with the cooked onions. Heat the mixture through and serve in a warmed dish.

Eggs with Onion Sauce

OEUFS À LA TRIPE

Serves 4

4 eggs
3 large onions, peeled and
  chopped (about 4 cups)

FOR THE SAUCE:
2 tbs. butter
1 tb. all-purpose flour
1 cup milk
pinch of nutmeg
2 tbs. minced parsley

Potato, Egg, and Herring Salad

SALADE BELLECOUR

Serves 4

4 medium potatoes, peeled and
   halved
⅔ cup dry white wine
1½ tbs. butter
2 chicken livers
1 tb. prepared mustard
¼ cup olive oil
4 eggs, hard-boiled and shelled
6 smoked herring fillets, chopped
2 tbs. fresh chopped chives,
   chervil, or parsley

This salad is much loved by the people of Lyons. It may be served either as an appetizer or as part of a cold lunch.

Cook the potatoes in boiling salted water for 12 minutes or until they are just tender. Drain and dry the potatoes, cut them into thick slices, and place on a deep plate or in a salad bowl. Sprinkle with white wine.

Melt the butter in a skillet and sauté the chicken livers for about 5 minutes, turning to brown on all sides. Mash them in a bowl. Add the mustard, oil, a dash of pepper, and mix well. Quarter the eggs and place them on the potatoes. Scatter the pieces of herring over the eggs and potatoes and pour the chicken-liver mixture over all. Sprinkle with the fresh herbs.

The black currant, a fruit often associated with Burgundy, is used to flavor liqueurs and is mixed with white wine to make a popular aperitif called Kir. In summer, ice cream is also made with black currants.

Crush the black currants with the back of a spoon through a sieve—preferably a conical fine-mesh strainer or chinois—and retain the juice. Discard the pulp. Blend the juice with the sifted confectioners sugar and the lemon juice. Beat the cream until it is thick. Then fold it into the black currant mixture. Pour the mixture into a large ice tray and freeze for about 2 hours or until it is firm. It is sometimes served with additional fresh cream, whipped with sugar.

Black Currant Ice Cream

GLACE AU CASSIS

Serves 6

4 cups black currants
2 cups sifted confectioners sugar
juice of ½ lemon
2 cups heavy cream

Honey Spice Cake

PAIN D'ÉPICES

Serves 8 to 10

1 lb. (1½ cups) thick honey
4 cups rye flour
pinch each of salt, dried ginger,
    and cinnamon
4 cloves, crushed
¼ cup milk
½ tsp. baking soda
3 eggs, lightly beaten

FOR THE FROSTING:
1 cup sifted confectioners sugar
1–2 tbs. lemon juice or kirsch
candied fruits for decoration

This French version of gingerbread is a specialty of Burgundy, Dijon in particular. Wrapped in foil and stored in a cool place, it keeps at least 2 weeks.

Warm the honey in a pan over very low heat, stirring constantly with a wooden spoon. Measure the flour into an earthenware bowl and make a well in the center. Add the honey, salt and spices. Mix and knead to a rough dough. Cover the dough with wax paper or a plastic bag to prevent drying. Let stand at room temperature for 24 hours.

Preheat the oven to 325.

Warm the milk. Dissolve the baking soda in it. Beat in the eggs, add the mixture to the dough, and mix well. Knead thoroughly for at least 10 minutes. The dough should be quite stiff and rough in texture. Spoon the dough into a well-greased loaf pan, 9½ by 5½ by 2½. Bake in the preheated oven for 1 hour 20 minutes or until a toothpick inserted into the cake comes out clean. Cool before removing from the pan.

Mix the confectioners sugar with the lemon juice or kirsch and stir well. Spread the mixture over the top of the cake and decorate with candied fruit.

Dauphiné and Savoy

This region stretches from the Alps to the Rhone Valley, from Switzerland down to Provence in the south. It has produced many of the greatest chefs of all time, as well as several famous writers on cooking, including Jean Anthelme Brillat-Savarin, who was born in Bellay on April 2, 1755. His *Physiologie du goût* (*Physiology of Taste*), an elegant and witty compendium on the art of dining, was published in 1825. Many of Brillat-Savarin's aphorisms are still cherished and quoted; among them are: "The fate of nations hangs upon their choice of food." "Tell me what you eat: I will tell you what you are." "Dessert without cheese is like a pretty woman with only one eye."

Dauphiné and Savoy are heavily traveled vacation areas. The Alps provide excellent winter skiing and a summer paradise for mountain climbers and devotees of water sports. Naturally, the luxury hotels and fine restaurants have been sufficiently influenced by vacationers to provide an international menu but the local inhabitants remain true to their traditional cuisine, which can best be described as hearty, satisfying, and healthful—typical of the cuisine of mountainous regions.

As in most French provinces, the basic ingredients are fine but perhaps not as varied as in some areas. However, the fish are delicious, and the lavaret, dace, and char are practically impossible to find anywhere other than Savoy. Trout are still plentiful, although trout fishing is now closely controlled. Pike, carp, and perch from this area have a delicate taste owing to the purity of the water. Savoy's superb *soupe aux poissons* is similar to *bouillabaisse* but made from freshwater fish. The regional game is tasty; thrushes gorge themselves on juniper berries, which are also added to a sauce in which they are cooked. The meat of the wild boar tastes of wild herbs, as does that of the hare and rabbit. Partridge, quail, and woodcock are also abundant, and frequently are made into pâtés.

The humble potato is part of Dauphiné and Savoy cooking. In fact, any dish described as *à la dauphinoise*, or as *à la savoyarde*, is likely to be accompanied by some variety of potato.

The Savoyard likes to cook with cream, cheese, and butter, mainly because excellent dairy produce is plentiful. In winter, skiers love to have a *fondue* or a *raclette* (melted cheese dishes), which they often eat in groups around a log fire. The cheeses of Savoy and Dauphiné are among the most varied and delicious in France. Beaufort, Persille, Reblochon, tomme au marc, and Vacherin are made of cows' milk; tomme de Praslin, tomme de Belley, Chevrotin, and Hauteluce are made of goats' milk. A Dauphiné or Savoy cheese *gratin* may contain almost anything: macaroni, meat, mushrooms, cardoons, even crayfish tails.

The forests of the Alps produce mushrooms which rival in excellence those of the Franche-Comté. They are gathered by connoisseurs who combine them with the simple cookery of the province to produce rich, sophisticated dishes.

The fruit crops of the region are of excellent quality. Plums, pears, and cider apples come from Savoy, and walnuts and chestnuts come from both the Savoy and Dauphiné. Perhaps the finest fruit to come from the Savoy is the *fraises des bois*, the tiny, wild strawberry from which the provincial housewife produces not only excellent jams, but also a delightful taste treat to accompany a light-as-air cake made from beaten egg whites and sugar.

This region is also known for candies, such as the renowned *nougat* made at Montélimar. *Noix de Grenoble* (sugared walnuts) are also widely appreciated throughout France. Dauphiné has a characteristic regional dessert, *pogne*, which appears in the south of the region as a huge *brioche* crown decorated with candied fruit, and in the north as a fruit or pumpkin pie. Almost every village and town has its own slightly different version. A special local dessert of the Savoy is *farçon*, made of sweetened white potatoes.

This mountainous region is also a country of vineyards. From Dauphiné comes the famous red wine l'Hermitage, and also the good red wines (some truly excellent) classed under the name "Côtes du Rhone Drome." The vineyards of Savoy date from the time of the Roman occupation. Neglected during the Dark Ages, they were reclaimed and the quality of the wine refined by monks during the Middle Ages. These white, very dry wines have a fine bouquet. The best known are undoubtedly those of Arbins, Montmélian, Roussette de Savoie, and the fine sparkling Mousseux. Dauphiné and Savoy also produce some fine spirits, such as Aiguebelle, brandy, and vermouth. Cherry ratafia is often made at home, and a medieval recipe is used to make a liqueur called Genepi, which is based on herbs and spices.

Chicken with Juniper

POULET AU GENIÈVRE

Serves 4

1 3-lb. chicken
12 dried juniper berries
6 tbs. butter
3 tbs. peanut oil
2 shallots, peeled and chopped
2 tbs. minced parsley
1¼ cups dry white wine
2 large potatoes, peeled and diced
   (about 4 cups)
⅓ cup gin
⅔ cup heavy cream

Juniper grows wild in the countryside of Dauphiné and Savoy, and it gives a pleasant taste to many sauces. This recipe is also suitable for such game birds as pheasant, partridge, and guinea fowl.

Cut the chicken into 8 pieces. Pound the juniper berries well, in a mortar if possible. Melt 4 tablespoons of the butter and 1½ tablespoons of the oil in a large shallow skillet. Add half the juniper berries and half the chopped shallots and parsley to the fat in the pan. As soon as the shallots turn slightly brown, add the pieces of chicken. Sauté them over high heat for 10 minutes, shaking the pan often and turning the pieces occasionally. If the chicken sticks to the pan, pour in a little white wine. When the chicken is golden, pour in ¾ cup of the white wine. Lower the heat, cover, and cook for 30 minutes.

Roll the potatoes in a cloth so they are perfectly dry. When the chicken has been cooking for about 20 minutes, heat the remaining butter and oil in a large skillet. Add the remaining shallot and parsley. Put all the diced potatoes into the skillet and flatten them a little, so they resemble a thick pancake. Add a seasoning of salt and pepper. Cook without stirring, pressing down as the potatoes soften. Turn the potatoes with a spatula. When golden brown on both sides, slide onto a large heated serving dish.

Season the chicken pieces with salt and pepper and lay them on top of the potatoes. Pound the remaining 6 juniper berries and add them to the pan in which the chicken was cooked, along with the rest of the white wine, gin, and cream. Stir briskly and heat almost to boiling, but do not boil. Pour the mixture over the pieces of chicken and serve immediately.

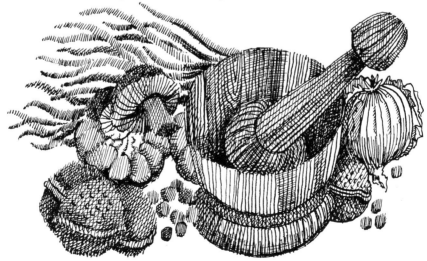

mortar and pestle

Mushroom Soufflé

SOUFFLÉ AUX
CHAMPIGNONS

Serves 4

1 lb. mushrooms
6 tbs. butter
pinch of nutmeg
3 tbs. all-purpose flour
⅔ cup milk
2 tbs. minced parsley
¼ tsp. dried thyme
6 egg yolks
5 egg whites
¾ cup grated Swiss cheese

In Savoy, this recipe is made with morels, but cultivated mushrooms may be substituted.

Preheat the oven to 350.

Clean the mushrooms with a damp paper towel. Trim and chop finely. Melt half the butter in a skillet and sauté the mushrooms. Add a seasoning of salt and pepper and a pinch of nutmeg. Stir in the flour and cook over high heat, stirring briskly, for 3 minutes. Add the milk, a little at a time, stirring constantly. As soon as the sauce comes to a boil and thickens, remove the pan from the heat and cool for a moment. Add the parsley and thyme. One by one, add the egg yolks, stirring after each addition. Beat the egg whites with a pinch of salt until they are stiff. Then fold them gently into the mushroom sauce, lifting the mixture rather than stirring it. Grease a 6-cup soufflé dish with the remaining butter. Pour in the mixture and sprinkle the top with the cheese. Bake in the preheated oven for 30 to 40 minutes, until the soufflé is well risen and the surface is golden brown. Serve at once.

Variations of this dish are eaten all over France. It is a specialty of Bugey in Savoy.

Preheat the oven to 300.

Heat ½ the butter in a skillet and brown the chicken livers. Sprinkle with the parsley and thyme and cook gently for 5 minutes, turning the livers. Puree the livers in an electric blender, adding a bit of the cream if your machine clogs. If you do not have a blender, mash the livers in a mortar. When smooth, place the livers in a mixing bowl. Add the cream, cornstarch, nutmeg, salt, and pepper, mixing well. Then add the egg yolks and mix well again. Beat the egg whites until they are very stiff and fold them into the mixture. Pour into a soufflé dish greased with the remaining butter and bake for 30 minutes. Serve immediately.

Chicken Liver Soufflé

SOUFFLÉ DE FOIES DE VOLAILLE

Serves 4

4 tbs. butter
6 chicken livers
1 tb. minced parsley
¼ tsp. dried thyme
1 cup heavy cream
1 tb. cornstarch
pinch of nutmeg
5 egg yolks
4 egg whites

Combination Salad

SALADE RHODANIENNE

Serves 4

3 large potatoes, peeled and halved
1 cup dry white wine
4 anchovy fillets in oil
½ bunch watercress, washed and trimmed
½ lb. dry sausage (saucisson or salami), diced
½ lb. smoked ham, diced
¼ lb. Swiss cheese, diced
½ cup green olives
¼ cup olive oil
1 tb. vinegar
few sprigs fresh chervil or parsley, chopped

This salad may be served either at the beginning or at the end of a meal. In summer, it is enough for a light lunch.

Place the potatoes in a pan of boiling water. Bring back to the boil, lower the heat, and cook for 12 minutes or until the potatoes are just tender. Drain, cool for a moment, and cut the potatoes into thick slices. Put these into a salad bowl and sprinkle with white wine and season with salt and pepper.

Cut the anchovy fillets into small pieces and add them to the salad bowl with the watercress, sausage, ham, cheese, and olives. Sprinkle with oil and vinegar, and then with the chervil or parsley.

> Nasturtium flowers are a colorful and tasty garnish for this salad. The leaves, the lovely orange and yellow flowers, and the seeds of Nasturtiums are often used in salads for their pungent taste and beautiful color.

Veal Olives

PAUPIETTES DE VEAU

Serves 4

4 thin veal scallops, about ¼ lb. each
pinch of cayenne pepper
¼ lb. small mushrooms
2 tbs. minced parsley
½ tsp. dried thyme
1 lb. lean veal, ground
1 egg
2 cups dried white bread crumbs
1 tsp. Cognac or brandy
1 tb. peanut oil
2 tbs. butter
3 shallots, peeled
1 cup dry white wine

Variations of this dish are made throughout France. In the Midi tomato puree and chopped olives are added along with a touch of garlic. In southwestern France the veal is often seasoned with chopped red peppers. The scallops should be pounded briefiy between sheets of waxed paper to a thickness of 1/4 inch.

Sprinkle the scallops with salt, pepper, and cayenne, and rub in well. Clean the mushrooms with a damp paper towel and chop them. In a mixing bowl, combine the mushrooms, parsley, thyme, and ground veal. Season with salt and pepper. Beat the egg and mix it with the bread crumbs. Combine with the mushroom-veal mixture. Add the Cognac. Put a tablespoon or two of this stuffing on each veal scallop. Roll each and tie with strong white twine, giving the veal rolls an elongated shape.

Heat the oil and butter in a saucepan, and lightly sauté the shallots. Discard them as soon as they are lightly colored. Place the veal rolls in the pan and brown them on all sides over moderate heat—about 5 minutes in all. Add half the white wine. Cover and cook gently for 15 minutes, shaking the pan from time to time. Add the rest of the white wine. Cook gently, uncovered, for an additional 15 minutes. Remove the twine and serve with noodles or boiled potatoes.

Chestnut Soup

SOUPE AUX
CHÂTAIGNES

Serves 6

2 lbs. fresh, or
   1 lb. canned chestnuts
1 celery stalk
2 cups milk
2 cups vegetable stock
pinch of nutmeg
⅔ cup Madeira
½ cup heavy cream

Sweet chestnuts are found in both Savoy and Dauphiné, and they are cooked in various ways. Fresh or canned chestnuts may be used to make this dish.

If you are using fresh chestnuts, slash them and place in a large saucepan. Cover with lightly salted water. Add the celery and simmer for 20 minutes. Drain the chestnuts and remove the shell and the inner skin.

If canned chestnuts are used, place in a strainer under cold running water to remove syrup and drain. Simmer with the celery for 10 to 15 minutes. Strain and proceed with recipe.

Replace chestnuts and celery in the saucepan; add the milk, stock, nutmeg, and pepper. Bring to a boil and simmer gently over low heat for about 30 minutes, or until the chestnuts are soft and can be mashed easily.

Remove the chestnuts and celery from the broth with a slotted spoon and pass them through the fine blade of a food mill. Return the puree to the broth.

Alternatively, you can puree the chestnuts in a blender, moistening them with a little of the stock.

Reheat the soup. Stirring constantly, add the Madeira and the cream. Heat through, but do not allow to boil.

Baked Potato and Egg Cake

FARÇON

Serves 6

8 large potatoes
¾ cup butter
pinch of nutmeg
1 cup milk
5 eggs
¼ cup sugar

This is an old Savoyard recipe. It can be served either as a first course or as a dessert.

Preheat the oven to 400.

Scrub the potatoes well but do not peel them. Dry them and bake for 45 minutes or until they are tender and well cooked. Raise the oven to 425. Peel and mash the potatoes while they are still hot. Add the butter in small pieces, and a seasoning of salt and pepper and nutmeg. Gradually add the milk, stirring well. Beat each egg separately and add them one by one. Finally, stir in the sugar. Butter a shallow 6-cup baking dish and pour in the mixture. Bake for 15 to 20 minutes or until the farcon is golden brown.

If crayfish are unavailable in your area, substitute shrimp or lobster in this recipe.

Wash and finely chop the carrots, shallots, and celery. Put them in a large saucepan, cover, and place the pan over high heat. Cook for a few seconds to draw out the juices, shaking the pan. Then add the wine, herbs, peppercorns, chili powder, and a pinch of salt. Bring quickly to a boil and cook uncovered until the wine is reduced by half. Add the fish and cook for 10 minutes. Strain the liquid. Arrange the fish on a heated serving dish and pour the strained liquid over the fish.

This recipe is suitable for any large fish. When buying pike choose a brightly colored one.

Make the marinade by combining in a large bowl the Madeira, Cognac, wine, peeled shallots, chopped celery, bay leaves, parsley, thyme, peppercorns, and a pinch of salt. Add the fish and leave overnight.

Preheat the oven to 400.

Transfer the fillets to a well-greased gratin or oval baking dish. Strain the marinade and pour it over the pike; if there is too much, reserve some. Clean the mushrooms with a damp paper towel, slice them thinly, and add to the pike. Place in the preheated oven and cook for 20 minutes, basting often. If necessary, add a little of the reserved marinade. When the fillets are cooked, carefully lift them out with a slotted spoon, and place them with the mushrooms on a hot serving dish. Return the fish to the turned-off oven to keep warm.

Mix the egg yolks and the cream in a saucepan. Add the cornstarch and 3 to 4 tablespoons of the liquid in which the fish was cooked. Bring to a boil. Pour the sauce over the fish and serve at once.

Crayfish in White Wine

ÉCREVISSES À LA NAGE

Serves 4

3 carrots
3 shallots, peeled
1 celery stalk
1 bottle dry white wine
2 bay leaves
sprig fresh, or ¼ tsp. dried thyme
6 peppercorns
pinch of chili powder
2 dozen crayfish, or 1½ lbs.
    shrimp or small lobster tails

Baked Pike in Cream Sauce

BROCHET MARINÉ À
L'ÉVIANAISE

Serves 4 to 6

1 2-lb. pike, filleted
¼ lb. mushrooms

FOR THE MARINADE:
⅔ cup Madeira
5 tbs. Cognac
2 cups dry white wine
3 shallots, peeled
1 celery stalk, chopped
2 bay leaves
few sprigs parsley
¼ tsp. dried thyme
6 peppercorns

FOR THE SAUCE:
2 egg yolks
1 cup heavy cream
1 tb. cornstarch

Flamed Stuffed Partridges

PERDREAUX FLAMBÉS

Serves 2

2 partridges, plucked, cleaned, and
   singed
½ lb. pâté or foie gras mousse
8 dried juniper berries, crushed
3 tbs. gin
¼ cup butter
¾ cup gin

Partridge has a particular affinity for juniper berries and gin, as this recipe will demonstrate. Count on one partridge per serving.

Preheat the oven to 400.

Stuff the partridges with a mixture of pâté or foie gras, crushed juniper berries, a seasoning of salt and pepper, and the gin. Place in the preheated oven for 20 to 30 minutes, basting 2 or 3 times with the butter. Alternatively, you can roast the birds on a spit for about 20 minutes. Place the partridges on a hot serving dish, warm the remaining gin, pour it over the birds, and, averting your face, ignite with a match. Serve immediately.

Creamed Potatoes

GRATIN DAUPHINOIS

Serves 4

3 large potatoes, peeled and thinly
   sliced (about 5 cups)
1 clove garlic, peeled
6 tbs. butter
pinch of nutmeg
1½ cups heavy cream

For a less rich _gratin dauphinois_, substitute milk for all or part of the cream.

At the end of the last century, many women of this region worked all day in factories. They would prepare this dish and leave it with the baker on their way to work. As they were going home for supper, they would collect it, hot and golden brown.

Preheat the oven to 450.

Dry the potato slices in a cloth. Rub the garlic around the inside of a baking dish. Butter the dish well, using a third of the butter, and arrange the potato slices in layers. Season the layers with salt, sprinkle the top lightly with nutmeg, and pour over the cream. Dot the remaining butter over the surface. Bake in the preheated oven for 10 minutes. Then lower the heat to 350 and cook for another hour.

Peaches in Brandy

PÊCHES À L'EAU-DE-VIE

Makes about 6 lbs.

24 ripe peaches
2¼ cups sugar
2 cups water
8 cloves
1 cinnamon stick, broken into
    small pieces
4 cups brandy

Delicious after a heavy meal, these peaches can also be used to enhance ice cream, fruit salads, and flans.

Prick the fruit in two or three places with a long needle. Add the peaches to a large saucepan of boiling water. Leave them for a minute and then remove with a slotted spoon. Rinse the peaches under cold running water. Peel them and let dry. Cut the peaches in half and place them in sterilized jars, filling the jars not more than three-quarters full.

In a saucepan, dissolve the sugar in the water. Bring to a boil and cook for 3 minutes. Pour the syrup over the peaches and add the cloves and the cinnamon. Let cool completely before covering with the brandy. Seal the jars and leave for 1 month before serving.

Ring Cake with Raspberries

COURONNE AUX FRAMBOISES

Serves 6

2 eggs
1 cup sugar
grated peel of ½ orange
¾ cup sweet white wine
⅓ cup peanut oil
2¼ cups sifted all-purpose flour
1 tb. baking powder

FOR THE FILLING:
2 cups raspberries
½ cup sugar
1 cup heavy cream

Many wild raspberries are found in the Alps. They have an unusual perfume. You can, of course, substitute cultivated raspberries, or even completely defrosted frozen raspberries.

Preheat the oven to 375.

Beat the whole eggs with the sugar and add the grated orange peel. Beat until the mixture is thick and pale yellow. Pour the wine and oil into the egg mixture and mix well. Add the sifted flour. Mix again and finally stir in the baking powder. Grease a 9-inch tube pan and pour in the batter. Bake in the center of the preheated oven for 35 minutes, or until the cake is risen and brown. Let the cake cool completely before removing it from the pan. Place the raspberries in the center of the cake. Dust with the sugar and cover with the cream—whipped, if desired.

Alsace and Lorraine

The people of Alsace and Lorraine have guarded and preserved their traditions in cooking, in customs, and even in dress, perhaps longer and more jealously than any other group in France.

Located in northeastern France, the regions of Alsace and Lorraine are geographically separated by the Vosges mountain chain. They are bound together historically, however, in that the French and the Germans have long contended for their territories. While this has resulted in cultural similarities between these two regions, they differ fundamentally in that Alsace is the most foreign territory of France. Its culture is essentially Germanic in origin, which accounts for its distinctive customs and language, Alsatian (which is a German dialect into which numerous French words have been borrowed). Virtually all Alsatians, however, speak French in addition to Alsatian. Lorraine, on the other hand, has remained more thoroughly French in culture.

The cooking in this region is excellent but not overly sophisticated. Most housewives still use the recipes of their ancestors, and some of the best recipes date from the Middle Ages. When a recipe survives the centuries, it is because it deserves to do so. Some recipes, such as those for game served with fruit sauce, are special to this area of France. Since there are no real agricultural specialties in this region, the cuisine of Alsace and Lorraine is not determined by the available raw materials to the extent that the cuisines of other regions of France are.

As is to be expected, German foods have heavily influenced the Alsatian cuisine, but the Alsatians have blended in French subtlety to temper the heaviness normally associated with German cookery. Alsace is noted for its *tarte à l'oignon,* and is equally famous for a variety of *choucroute* (sauerkraut). Just what the *choucroute* is cooked with depends upon the cook: pork, ham, sausage, boiled potatoes, smoked goose, and partridge are some possible ingredients. Chicken *vol-au-vent*, made with cream sauce in a pastry shell, is another popular dish. There is also a light cake, called *gugelhupf*, which the Alsatians eat with coffee at any time of the day—including for breakfast.

Pork dishes are also popular in Alsace. Two traditional favorites are *porcelet farci à la peau de goret*, roast stuffed suckling pig, and *schifela*, pork shoulder with bitter turnips. Other Alsatian specialties include smoked ham, smoked sausage with caraway, *knackwurst* (little sausages), and *leberwurst* (a creamy-textured liver sausage). Strasbourg produces the incomparable, internationally renowned *pâté de foie gras* with truffles.

The soups of Alsace are basic and tasty. *Consommé à l'alsacienne* is a combination of sauerkraut and sliced sausage in consommé. Flour soup (a hot consommé of flour paste, nutmeg, heavy cream, and butter) and onion soup are also traditional.

The fish of Alsace are fine, particularly the salmon, trout, pike, carp, and crayfish. Dumplings, noodles, cabbage, and asparagus are important parts of the Alsace cuisine.

Besides the *gugelhupf* already mentioned, favorite Alsatian desserts include *tarte alsacienne*, a custard and fruit tart, *birwecka*, a rich cake, and *kaffee krantz*, coffee cake.

Lorraine is best known for its *quiche Lorraine*, a pastry with a cream and beaten-egg filling that includes bits of bacon and sometimes cheese and onion. *Potée Lorraine*, another popular dish, consists of pork, carrots, turnips, leeks, cabbage, and sausage. A whole range of pork products comes from Lorraine, including the famous blood sausage of Nancy. Other traditional favorites include partridge and cabbage, and cold suckling pig in jelly.

The most popular Lorraine pastry is *ramequin*, a sweet flour-and-milk cake. *Madeleines* is a spongy type of cupcake. Some excellent jams and jellies come from the region, as do Jordan almonds.

The vineyards of the region produce some fine wines; the best known are Sylvaner, Riesling, Gewürztraminer, White Pinot, and Gray Pinot (nicknamed the "Tokay of Alsace"). The hillside orchards produce splendid fruits that are used for liqueurs (such as *kirsch*, *quetsche*, *mirabelle*, and *framboise*) as well as for jams, candied fruits, and preserves, which are exported all over the world.

And we must not forget the cheese! There are plenty of local cheeses to give a perfect finishing touch to a good meal: Carré de l'Est, Gerôme, Gerôme with anise seed, Münster (sometimes flavored with caraway), and Recollet, as well as less-known products of local farms.

Onion Soup

SOUPE À L'OIGNON

Serves 4

3 large onions
¼ cup butter
3 tbs. all-purpose flour
1½ qts. beef stock or
    canned beef bouillon
12 slices French bread
2 cups grated Swiss cheese

This popular soup is very easy to prepare, and it is delicious.

Peel the onions (under running water so that they do not make you weep) and either chop finely, grate, or pass them through a food mill. You should have about 8 cups. Melt the butter in a large saucepan. Add the onions and sauté until they become soft and transparent, but not brown. Sprinkle with flour and cook over low heat for 1 minute, stirring briskly with a wooden spoon. Stirring constantly, gradually pour in the stock. Bring to a boil. Then lower the heat so the soup just simmers, and cook for 30 minutes. Toast the slices of bread and serve them in the soup. Serve the grated cheese separately.

> To improve the flavor of canned bouillon (canned consommé is not recommended at all because it is too sweet) simmer 2 cups of undiluted bouillon for 20 minutes with ½ cup red wine or dry white wine, 3 tbs. each of minced carrots, onions, and celery, 2 parsley sprigs, ⅓ bay leaf, and ⅛ tsp. dried thyme.

Quiche Lorraine

QUICHE LORRAINE

Serves 4

FOR THE PASTRY:
1½ cups sifted all-purpose flour
½ cup butter
6 tbs. cold water

FOR THE FILLING:
10 slices bacon
2 eggs
3 egg yolks
2 cups heavy cream

This is probably the most famous recipe from Lorraine, but it is also made throughout France. It can be served as a first course, or as the main course of a light meal. The people of Lorraine like to eat it for breakfast.

Place the sifted flour in a bowl. Add the butter in small pieces, and blend it into the flour using your fingertips. Stir in the water, and a pinch of salt. Knead to a dough. Shape the dough into a ball and let stand for 1 hour, covered with a cloth.

Preheat the oven to 400.

Roll out the dough thinly into a circle on a floured board. Grease a 9-inch quiche mold or pie plate and line it with pastry. Trim the edges with your fingertips. Press all around the inside of the rim with the tines of a fork. Prick the bottom of the dough at regular intervals so that it is dotted with tiny holes. Arrange the bacon slices, trimmed, if necessary, over the bottom. Place in the preheated oven for 10 minutes. Then remove from the oven. Beat the eggs, egg yolks, and cream together. It is not necessary to add salt, as the bacon is already salty, but add pepper lavishly from a mill. Pour the mixture over the bacon and return the quiche to the oven for an additional 30 minutes. Serve hot.

Garnished Sauerkraut

CHOUCROUTE GARNIE

Serves 4

2 tbs. lard or goose fat
1 onion, peeled and chopped
    (about ¾ cup)
1¼ lbs. sauerkraut
⅔ cup dry white wine
10 dried juniper berries
1 baking apple, peeled, cored, and
    chopped
3 cups chicken stock or canned
    chicken broth
1 lb. bacon in one piece, soaked
    overnight
4 small pork chops
8 potatoes
¼ cup kirsch
8 frankfurters

Before cooking, drain and soak
the sauerkraut in 3–4 changes
of cold water for about ½ hour.
This is done to remove the taste
of the preserving brine.

This is one of the best known Alsatian dishes. In Alsace, it is often put on to cook before going to church on Sunday morning and served as a substantial midday dinner.

Use an earthenware pot, protected from the heat with an asbestos mat, or a large heavy casserole. Melt the lard or goose fat in the casserole. Add the onion and brown it. Stir in the sauerkraut and add the white wine, preferably one from Alsace. Crush the juniper berries in a mortar or with the back of a spoon. (Juniper berries have a stronger taste when used crushed rather than whole.) Add them along with the apple to the pot and stir in the stock. Cover the casserole and cook very slowly for 3 hours.

Add the bacon and pork chops. Cover and cook for an additional 30 minutes.

Meanwhile, wash and scrub the potatoes, but do not peel them. Cook for 15 to 20 minutes in boiling water.

Add the kirsch to the sauerkraut and cook, uncovered, for 10 minutes. Prick the frankfurters with a fork so that they do not burst, and put them into a pan of boiling water. Cook them over low heat for about 10 minutes. Remove the bacon from the pot and slice it. Spoon the sauerkraut into the middle of a large, heated serving dish. Lay the pork chops, bacon, and frankfurters on top. Surround with the potatoes and serve.

Perch with Cream

PERCHES À LA CRÈME

Serves 4

4 small perch, each weighing about
    ½ lb., scaled and cleaned
juice of 1 lemon
¾ cup all-purpose flour
¼ cup butter
½ bottle dry white wine
2 shallots, peeled and chopped
1¾ cups heavy cream
2 tbs. minced parsley

This recipe may be used for most freshwater fish. Serve as a first course or as a main dish with steamed potatoes, and the same Rhine wine used in preparing the recipe.

Preheat the oven to 400.

Sprinkle the fish with the lemon juice and coat with flour. Lavishly butter an ovenproof dish and arrange the fish on it. Cook for 15 minutes in the preheated oven. Drain off as much of the melted butter as possible. Then pour in the white wine. Add the shallots. Return the dish to the oven for 10 minutes, after which remove and pour the cream over the fish and sprinkle with parsley. Season with salt and pepper. Return the dish to the oven for a further 3 to 5 minutes to heat through.

Every wine-growing region in France seems to have its own version of chicken stewed in wine.

Cut the bird into 8 pieces and dry thoroughly.

Heat the butter and oil in a heavy pan. Add the shallots, parsley, and thyme. When the shallots begin to turn golden brown, add the chicken pieces. Sauté them over high heat, adjusting the heat so the fat does not burn, until they are browned on all sides. This step will take 5 to 10 minutes.

Remove the pan from the heat. Pour in the warmed Cognac and, averting your face, ignite it with a match. Shake the pan to spread the flames. When the flames have died, slowly pour in the white wine. Bring to a boil. Then lower the heat and add the sugar, nutmeg, and salt and pepper to taste.

Cover and cook gently over low heat for about 25 minutes. Lift out the pieces of chicken and place them on a heated serving dish. Strain the sauce and return it to the pan. Mix the cornstarch with the cream and the lemon juice. Stir the paste into the hot sauce and bring to a boil, stirring constantly. Pour the sauce over the chicken and serve.

❦

This salad is excellent as a first course, at the end of a meal, or as an accompaniment to roast pork or boiled beef. To develop its flavor, it should be prepared several days before it is served.

Wash and dry the cabbage. Remove the outer leaves, cut away the core, and shred finely. Put a layer of the shredded cabbage into a jar, ideally a deep stone jar. Cover with a layer of salt. Add another layer of cabbage and then one of salt. Place the onion in the center. Continue with the layers until all the cabbage has been used, and finish with a layer of salt. Cover and let stand in a cool place for 24 hours. Then drain off the water produced by the cabbage and add the vinegar. Cover and leave in a cool place for several days, preferably 10 to 12.

Before using, drain and rinse the cabbage in a sieve, and remove the onion stuck with cloves. Place in a salad bowl. Season with pepper and sprinkle with oil. Stir well and garnish with capers.

Chicken in White Wine

COQ AU VIN BLANC

Serves 4

1 3-lb. frying chicken
2 tbs. butter
3 tbs. peanut oil
3 shallots, peeled and chopped
3 tbs. minced parsley
½ tsp. dried thyme
¼ cup Cognac
1 bottle dry white wine
1 tsp. sugar
pinch of nutmeg
1 tb. cornstarch
3 tbs. heavy cream
juice of 1 lemon

This dish should be prepared with one of the refreshing white Alsatian wines such as Traminer or Riesling. A bottle of the same wine would go well with the dinner.

Red Cabbage Salad

SALADE DE CHOU ROUGE

Serves 6

1 large red cabbage
about ½ lb. coarse (kosher) salt
1 large onion, peeled and stuck with 4 cloves
1 cup wine vinegar
¼ cup peanut oil
¼ cup capers, drained (optional)

Onion Tart

TARTE À L'OIGNON

Serves 6

FOR THE PASTRY:
1½ cups sifted all-purpose flour
½ cup butter
6 tbs. water
1 egg, beaten, for glazing

FOR THE FILLING:
6 tbs. butter
3 large onions, peeled and chopped
    (about 5½ cups)
pinch of ground caraway seeds
4 eggs
¾ cup heavy cream or
    sour cream

Liver Dumplings

QUENELLES DE FOIE

Serves 4

½ lb. pork liver
¼ lb. calf's liver
1 large onion, peeled and chopped
    (about 1 scant cup)
1 clove garlic, crushed
5 slices bacon, diced
3 eggs, beaten
5 tbs. all-purpose flour
large pinch of nutmeg
6 tbs. butter
½ cup grated Swiss or parmesan
    cheese
2 tbs. minced parsley

This is a specialty of Strasbourg, though it is found throughout Alsace. It is suitable as a first course for dinner and as a luncheon or supper dish. It can be made in advance and reheated.

Place the sifted flour in a bowl. Add the butter in small pieces and blend it into the flour using your fingertips. Stir in the water and a pinch of salt. Knead to a dough. Shape the dough into a ball and let stand for at least 30 minutes, covered with a cloth.

Roll out the dough thinly into a circle on a floured board. Line a greased 8-inch springform pan with the dough. Press the dough in neatly, particularly around the sides, and trim the edge. Brush the egg all over the dough, paying particular attention to the sides.

Preheat the oven to 400.

In a skillet melt the 6 tablespoons of butter. Sauté the onions. Season with salt and pepper and sprinkle with caraway. Cook over low heat until the onions are soft and transparent. Then remove the pan from the heat. Lightly beat the eggs with the cream over low heat and stir, without boiling, for about 1 minute. Pour the mixture into the prepared pastry. Bake in the preheated oven for 20 to 30 minutes. Serve hot or warm.

❧

These quenelles can be served in soup, as a main course for a light meal, or separately as a first course.

Chop the livers finely. Combine them with the onion, garlic, and bacon, and pass the mixture through a meat grinder or food mill. Add the beaten eggs, flour, nutmeg, and a seasoning of salt and pepper. Mix well.

Preheat the broiler.

Bring a large saucepan of lightly salted water to a boil. Reduce the heat and keep the water at a simmer. Drop the quenelle mixture by tablespoons into the water. Cook only a few at a time. The quenelles are cooked when they rise to the surface. Drain on paper towels and place them, one by one, in a lightly buttered ovenproof dish. Continue poaching and draining until the mixture is used up. Dot with the remaining butter. Sprinkle with the grated cheese and then the chopped parsley. Broil quickly to brown.

Plum Pie

TARTE AUX QUETSCHES

Serves 4

1½ cups sifted all-purpose flour
4–5 tbs. water
½ cup butter, softened

FOR THE FILLING:
1½ lbs. purple plums
4 unsweetened zwieback crackers
1 cup sugar
¼ teaspoon nutmeg

Quetsches are purple plums. They are used a great deal in Lorraine for tarts and brandy.

Measure the sifted flour into a bowl and make a well in the center. Add the water and a pinch of salt. Mix with your fingertips and then add the butter. Mix to a smooth dough. Shape into a ball and let stand in a cool place.

Preheat the oven to 400.

Pit the plums. Crush the crackers to crumbs, either in a mortar or in an electric blender. Roll the pastry into a circle on a floured board. Grease a 9-inch tart mold or pie plate and line it with the pastry. Trim the edges neatly and mark with a fork. Sprinkle with the crumbs. Arrange the plums on top. Then sprinkle with the sugar and nutmeg. Bake in the preheated oven for about 20 minutes. Serve warm.

❧

Alsatian Cake

GUGELHUPF

Serves 8 to 12

4 cups sifted all-purpose flour
1½ packages dry yeast
1 cup lukewarm milk
4 eggs
¾ cup plus 2 tbs. butter, softened
1 tsp. salt
½ cup sugar
1½ cups raisins
1 cup blanched, chopped almonds
½ cup sifted confectioners sugar

To blanch almonds drop the shelled nuts into boiling water for 1 minute. Drain and slip off the skin. Dry them for 5 minutes in a 350-degree oven. They can be chopped at high speed in the blender for a few seconds.

Gugelhupf is a famous Alsatian cake. This particular recipe comes from a great pastry cook in Colmar, Monsieur Jean. If possible, bake in a fluted gugelhupf tin, though a tube pan will do.

Put a quarter of the sifted flour in a bowl and mix in the yeast and lukewarm milk. Cover with a cloth and put the bowl in a warm place to prove the yeast. Let stand for about 2 hours, or until the dough has risen and doubled in volume. Add the rest of the flour and the eggs, one at a time, beating well after each addition. Add the softened butter and the salt. Knead until the dough comes away from the sides of the bowl. Then add the sugar and knead again.

Grease an 8-inch gugelhupf tin or tube pan and sprinkle the raisins and chopped almonds lightly over the bottom and sides of the tin. Add the dough (it should half fill the tin) and leave in a warm place for 1½ to 2 hours.

Preheat the oven to 350.

The dough should have risen to fill the tin. Bake for 1 hour in the preheated oven. Cool completely before removing the gugelhupf from the tin or pan. Dust with confectioners sugar.

Ile-de-France and Champagne

Paris can well be called the gastronomic center of the world; few are the dishes that cannot be tasted in this capital city, the heart of the Ile-de-France. The restaurants offer specialties from every region of France—indeed, from the whole world—and the shops are full of foods brought from the four corners of the earth.

But, like all the other districts of France, the Ile-de-France has its own traditional recipes based on regional produce. The countryside provides excellent fruits and vegetables of which the best known and most sought after are asparagus, button mushrooms, white beans, young peas, string beans, cauliflower, carrots, artichokes, cherries, strawberries, and peaches. Game is still to be found in the forest, and Ardennes thrushes, in particular, are prized by connoisseurs. Excellent pork contributes substantially to the fare, and freshwater fish are abundant.

A partial list of the region's typical dishes makes the mouth water: *boeuf à la ficelle, gratinée des Halles, entrecôte Bercy, pommes de terre soufflées, matelote* (pieces of freshwater fish cooked in wine with onions and mushrooms), and *crêpes Suzette* (those delicious thin pancakes served flaming in a liqueur mixture).

Other specialties include game, meat, and poultry pâtés, and delicious dishes of fried mixed small fish from the shores of the Marne.

The Ile-de-France is famous for its soups: *potage Saint-Germain*, a thick pea soup, *potage parisienne*, a mixed vegetable soup with potatoes, *potage Parmentier*, a thick potato soup, and a delicious asparagus soup from Argenteuil.

Several towns have their own sweet specialties: cakes from Compiègne, rose preserves from Provins, and sugared almonds from Melun.

The remarkable versatility of Parisian cooking is shown in pastry kitchens which produce magnificient creations such as *croquembouche,* a pyramid of pastry puffs, filled with cream and glazed with crystallized sugar. And who but a Parisian chef could produce a *charlotte Russe,* a *gâteau Saint-Honoré,* or *petits fours* served in a spun sugar basket?

Although the quality of the food is the primary concern of any highly rated chef, these Parisian artists are in no way unmindful of the theatrical effect of a flaming *crêpe* or a magnificent swan carved from ice as a buffet centerpiece. In the Parisian's kitchen the eye dictates excellence to the same degree as the palate.

Pastries and cakes are a specialty of the Champagne region. Cookies and spiced bread come from Reims, croquettes from Bau-sur-Aube, and sugared almonds from Châlons-sur-Marne. Ile-de-France and Champagne also produce some of the best of the great French cheeses. The Ile-de-France has Brie from Melun and Meaux, soft cream cheese from Coulommiers, and many local cheeses seldom found outside this region.

But the real glory of Champagne is, of course, the wines. They have always been excellent, but didn't make history until the seventeenth century, when the monk Dom Perignon was able to "champagniser" the wines of this region, making them frothy, dry, and sparkling all at the same time. Only wines treated in this way in the Champagne district have the right to this name. Because the vineyards can scarcely manage to satisfy the ever increasing demand, many little villages have disappeared to make way for more vines.

Champagne is available in several different sizes, the most common is called the bottle and holds 27 fluid ounces. There is also the magnum, which is equal to two bottles, and the Jeroboam or double magnum, which holds four bottles. There are several other, larger sizes, rarely found commercially, which hold 12, 16, and 20 bottles. The shape of the champagne bottle is noticably different from other wine bottles—it is much heavier, because a good deal of the fermentation takes place in the bottle and thinner glass would shatter under the pressure.

Opening a champagne bottle requires some skill in order to avoid spilling much of the contents. The best method is to wrap a towel or napkin around the neck of the bottle, then, holding it at a 45-degree angle pointed away from yourself or anyone else, grasp the cork firmly in one hand and twist the bottle with the other. This should result in the cork coming out easily, with very little spillage. If for some reason the cork refuses to budge, gently nudge it out by pressing your thumb against it while slowly rotating the bottle. One note of caution: Once the foil and wire have been removed, it is possible for the cork to blow out simply from the pressure inside the bottle. Therefore, it is recommended that the wire not be removed until you are ready to open and serve the wine.

Champagne has a special quality; a magic that evokes memories of celebrations—New Year's Eve, a wedding, or a bon voyage. And it is typical of the French that they would produce a wine of such special quality that the christening of a baby or a ship demands it's presence.

Deep-Fried Small Fish

FRITURE DE LA MARNE

Serves 4

2 lbs. whitebait or other very small
    fish, such as smelts
2 cups milk
1½ cups all-purpose flour
oil for deep-frying
4 tbs. minced parsley
2 lemons, cut into wedges

Around Paris, and especially in the valley of the Marne, the little riverside inns serve a friture on Sunday. It is a pleasant way to start a meal.

Wash the fish in plenty of water and place them in a colander to drain. Soak the fish in the milk for about 30 minutes, turning them occasionally. Drain the fish again and coat with flour. Lower the fish into a deep fryer of very hot oil and fry, turning, until they are golden. If you use a shallow skillet instead of a deep one, fry a few fish at a time. Season with salt and pepper. Sprinkle with chopped parsley and serve with lemon wedges.

Cream of Pea Soup

POTAGE CRÈME SAINT-GERMAIN

Serves 6

4 cups water
3½–4 lbs. fresh peas, shelled (about
    4 cups)
2 heads lettuce
1 leek
1 tsp. sugar
¼ cup butter
1 cup heavy cream
3 egg yolks
few sprigs fresh chervil or parsley,
    chopped

Though you will lose some delicacy of flavor, canned peas can be used in this recipe. Run cold water over them and drain before using.

Measure the water into a large saucepan and bring to a boil. Rinse the peas. Separate the lettuce, trim the bottom and the green tops of the leek. Wash both lettuce and leek thoroughly. Add the peas, lettuce, leek, sugar, salt, and pepper to the boiling water. Cook over medium heat for 30 minutes. Strain and reserve the liquid. Pass the vegetables through a food mill or sieve to make a puree, or puree them in a blender with a little of the reserved cooking liquid.

Heat the butter in a saucepan, add the puree, and stir for a few moments to blend with the butter. Gradually stir in enough of the reserved liquid to make a light soup. Heat gently. Blend the cream and egg yolk in a soup tureen and stir in the hot soup, a little at a time. Return the soup to the saucepan just for a moment to heat through. Do not boil or even simmer. Replace in the tureen, sprinkle with chopped chervil or parsley and serve at once.

Onion Soup Gratiné

GRATINÉE DES HALLES

Serves 4

¾ cup butter
3 large yellow onions, thinly sliced
   (about 5 cups)
1 French bread
2 cups grated Swiss cheese
1 cup beef stock or
   canned beef bouillon
2 tbs. minced parsley
¼ tsp. dried thyme
1 cup dry white wine

This delicious soup was for many years the traditional late night snack served in Les Halles, the central market of Paris. The market has been modernized and moved to the suburbs, but the soup is still a great treat.

Melt a third of the butter in a heavy saucepan and add the onions. Cook over a low heat, stirring occasionally, until the onions are golden brown, about 30 minutes.

Meanwhile, slice the bread, toast the slices, and spread them liberally with the remaining butter. Line individual ovenproof soup dishes with the rounds of toast. Sprinkle with half the Swiss cheese.

Place the stock, parsley, and thyme in the saucepan with the onions and bring to a boil. Pour in the white wine and heat but do not reboil.

Spoon the cooked onions over the slices of toast in the soup dishes. Pour in enough stock to moisten the toast. Sprinkle with the remaining cheese and place the soup dishes under a preheated broiler for a minute—just until the cheese is golden brown.

Peas in Cream Sauce

PETITS POIS À LA BOURGEOISE

Serves 6

1 head lettuce
¼ cup butter
3 lbs. fresh peas, shelled (about 3
   cups)
few sprigs parsley, tied together
⅓ cup water
1 tsp. sugar
½ cup heavy cream
2 egg yolks

This recipe dates from the time of Louis XV, when peas were considered a very exotic vegetable.

Wash and quarter the lettuce. Melt the butter in a heavy saucepan and add the peas. Sauté them for a few moments, shaking the pan constantly. Add the lettuce, parsley, and water. To keep the temperature low in the traditional manner, cover the pan with a soup plate filled with cold water. As the water in the soup plate becomes hot, replace it with cold water. Cook the peas very slowly for 1 hour, adding a little extra water to the saucepan if necessary. Add the sugar and a pinch of salt and continue to simmer gently for a few minutes.

Blend the cream and egg yolks together in a bowl. Add the mixture to the peas and heat, stirring constantly. Do not boil. Remove the parsley and serve at once.

The name Bercy comes from the great wine vaults of Paris. Hence, a Bercy sauce is a wine sauce. This recipe is typical of Paris and should be prepared with white wine.

Begin by making the sauce. Simmer the wine, shallots, carrot, thyme, bay leaf, salt, and pepper until the wine is reduced by half. When the wine is reduced, season the steaks and cook them for 4 or 5 minutes per side in hot butter in a skillet.

While the steaks are cooking, remove the sauce from the heat. Strain it, discard the vegetables and return to the pan. Cut the butter into small pieces and off heat beat the butter into the sauce with a wire whisk. Pour over the steaks and serve immediately.

❧

In France, small cultivated mushrooms are called Paris mushrooms. In fact, they are grown around Paris and also in Champagne. Any type of mushroom is suitable for this delicious appetizer.

Trim the stems and wipe the mushrooms with a damp paper towel. Melt half the butter in a skillet, add the mushrooms, and sauté quickly for 1 minute. Season with salt and pepper, cover, and cook gently for a few minutes until the mushroom juices begin to run. Sprinkle the flour and parsley into the pan and stir briskly. Cook for 1 minute, then stir in the cream. Cook for an additional few moments without boiling before adding the remaining butter and the lemon juice. Simmer gently, uncovered, while preparing the rolls. Slice the rolls in half and toast them. Butter them and arrange them on a hot plate. Spoon the mushrooms in the cream sauce over the rolls, and serve.

> When buying mushrooms make sure they are smooth and unblemished. The underside should be closed—when the gills are exposed the mushroom darkens and dries. Most of the intense flavor lies in the skin, so mushrooms should not be peeled or soaked. Always clean them by wiping with a damp paper towel.

Steak with White Wine Sauce

ENTRECÔTE BERCY

Serves 4

4 small steaks, 1 inch thick
3 tbs. butter

FOR THE BERCY SAUCE:
2 cups dry white wine
3 shallots, peeled and chopped
1 carrot, sliced
sprig fresh, or pinch of dried thyme
1 bay leaf
¼ cup butter

Creamed Mushrooms on Toast

CROÛTES AUX CHAMPIGNONS

Serves 4

1 lb. small mushrooms
¼ cup butter
1 tsp. all-purpose flour
1 tb. minced parsley
1 cup heavy cream
juice of 1 lemon
4 round soft rolls
3 tbs. butter

Braised Beef

BOEUF À LA MODE

Serves 4

1 calf's foot or foreshank
3 tbs. lard of 1¼ tbs. butter and
   1 tb. oil
2 lbs. pot roast of beef—chuck or
   rump in 1 piece
¼ cup white wine, dry or sweet
1 cup water
1 slice bacon
2 shallots, peeled and stuck with
   2 cloves each
bouquet garni
¼ teaspoon pepper
6 carrots, sliced
10 small or 2 large onions, peeled

Boeuf à la mode is a traditional dish of everyday French cooking. Eaten hot, cold, or reheated, it is delicious.

Wash the calf's foot and place it in rapidly boiling water for 5 minutes. Remove from the water and set it aside. Melt the lard (or the butter and oil) in an earthenware casserole protected from the heat by an asbestos mat, or in large heavy casserole, and lightly brown the beef. Mix the white wine and water and pour over the beef, making sure the liquid covers the meat. Add more water mixed with white wine, if necessary. If you choose a dry wine rather than a sweet one, add 1 teaspoon of sugar.

Add the bacon, shallots, bouquet garni, calf's foot, salt, and pepper to the casserole. Bring to a boil, lower the heat, and partially cover. Simmer gently for 2 hours, then add the carrots and onions (quartered if large ones are used).

Cook for another hour over low heat. Then remove and discard the calf's foot, the shallots stuck with cloves, the bouquet garni, and the bacon. Slice the beef and serve hot with boiled potatoes or macaroni. If you prefer the beef cold, put it in a bowl with the broth in the refrigerator until the broth sets to a firm jelly.

This is a luxurious recipe, though only a quarter of a bottle of champagne is used. Do not substitute a sparkling wine for the champagne—it will most likely be too sweet. If you must make a substitution, choose a light, dry white wine.

Melt the butter in a skillet, add the chopped shallots and, immediately after, the trout. Cook over high heat for 5 or 6 minutes, turning carefully once with a spatula and shaking the skillet from time to time. The trout should be golden. Remove the fish from the skillet and place them on a hot serving dish. Season with salt and pepper. Discard the butter and the shallots.

Heat the champagne in the empty skillet, but do not allow it to boil. Pour the champagne over the trout. Sprinkle with chervil and serve at once.

Trout in Champagne

TRUITES AU CHAMPAGNE

Serves 4

5 tbs. butter
2 shallots, peeled and chopped
4 small trout, cleaned, washed, and dried
¼ bottle champagne
few sprigs chopped chervil

127

Eggs Poached in White Wine

OEUFS À LA CHAMPENOISE

Serves 4

2 tbs. butter
1½ cups Swiss cheese, thinly
   sliced
⅓ cup dry white wine
pinch of nutmeg
2 tbs. minced parsley
4 eggs

Rabbit with Mustard Sauce

LAPIN DE GARENNE EN
SAUCE MOUTARDE

Serves 6

1 3½-lb. rabbit, skinned and cut
   into serving pieces
¼ cup prepared mustard
2 tbs. soft butter
½ tsp. dried thyme

FOR THE SAUCE:
3 tbs. butter
5 tbs. all-purpose flour
⅓ cup water
1 cup beef stock or
   canned beef bouillon
1 clove garlic, crushed
2 bay leaves
½ tsp. vinegar

This is an appetizing and quickly prepared lunch or dinner dish. Brie, cut in thin slices, is sometimes used instead of Swiss cheese.

Melt the butter in a gratin dish or shallow ovenproof casserole. Add the cheese and then the white wine. Heat gently, stirring constantly until the cheese melts. Add nutmeg, minced parsley, and pepper. Cook for a moment, then gently break the eggs into the dish. When they are almost cooked, put the casserole under the broiler for 1 minute. Serve in the dish.

Rabbit is very much like chicken, though the meat is firmer. Marinating it overnight in 1/3 cup of red wine vinegar, 1/4 cup olive oil, sliced onions, and garlic cloves will give it an excellent flavor.

Preheat oven to 350.

If you have marinated the rabbit, dry the pieces on paper towels before proceeding with the recipe. Coat the pieces of rabbit with the mustard and butter, then sprinkle them with thyme. Season with salt and pepper and place the pieces in a baking dish. Cook uncovered for 45 minutes to 1 hour in the preheated oven, turning the rabbit pieces from time to time.

While the rabbit is cooking, prepare the sauce. Heat the butter in a small saucepan and, as soon as it begins to foam, sprinkle in the flour, stirring rapidly. Add the water and stock, a little at a time, stirring constantly. Add the garlic and the bay leaves. Cover and cook slowly for about 20 minutes. Season with salt and pepper and then the vinegar. Spoon the sauce over the rabbit and serve immediately.

Mustard is an ancient condiment known to the Egyptians and introduced by the Romans to Gaul. The plants grown from the seeds brought by the Romans were particularly successful in Burgundy. Dijon, the capital of Burgundy, became the greatest mustard-producing center in France, perhaps the world. Today, Dijon's annual production of mustard exceeds 8,000 tons. In Dijon, the flavor of the mustard seed is brought out by the tart quality of the juice of the underripe grapes in which flour made from the seeds is dissolved. This paste is the Dijon mustard prized by gourmets.

Garnished Steaks with Béarnaise Sauce

TOURNEDOS HENRI IV

Serves 6

FOR THE GARNISH:
6 artichoke hearts
½ cup butter
2 large potatoes
1 tb. oil
6 slices white bread

FOR THE BÉARNAISE SAUCE:
2-3 shallots, peeled and chopped
1 tb. minced fresh, or
    ½ tsp. dried tarragon
⅓ cup dry white wine
⅓ cup wine vinegar
6 egg yolks
1 cup butter

FOR THE STEAK:
¼ cup butter
6 fillet steaks
1 tb. oil

Béarnaise sauce is basically an emulsion of butter in slightly cooked egg yolks. It is not difficult to make a successful béarnaise sauce if you heat the eggs very gently and add the butter slowly. Béarnaise sauce is served tepid and any attempt to heat it beyond that point will almost certainly result in its separating. If the finished sauce does start to separate, beat in a tablespoon of cold water.

Tournedos are small steaks taken from the heart of a fillet of beef. They are about 1 inch thick and 2 1/2 inches in diameter. The following recipe is a classic.

Prepare the garnish first. Cook fresh artichoke hearts in boiling water until they are tender. If using canned or frozen artichoke hearts, rinse them thoroughly in cold water before lowering them for a minute into boiling water. They are fragile and care must be taken not to break them. Drain, dry on paper towels, and sauté them lightly in 2 tablespoons of the butter. Sprinkle with salt and pepper. Peel and wash the potatoes and shape them into small balls, about the size of hazelnuts (a melon scoop is useful for this). You should have about 3½ cups of potato balls. Scald the potatoes by cooking them for 2 minutes in boiling salted water. Drain, then dry them in a dish towel, and brown them in a skillet in 2 tablespoons butter and the oil. Sprinkle with salt and pepper. Keep the artichoke hearts and potatoes hot in an unlit warm oven.

To prepare the béarnaise sauce, boil the shallots, tarragon, wine, and vinegar over moderate heat until the liquid is reduced by half. Remove the pan from the heat and cool. Add the egg yolks, one by one, stirring well after each addition. Season well with salt and pepper, and stir again. Over very low heat add the butter, little by little, in small pieces, stirring constantly with a wooden spoon. Once the sauce begins to thicken, the butter may be added more rapidly. Place the pan containing the béarnaise in a bain-marie to keep warm.

Cut off the crusts and corners of the bread and sauté in 4 tablespoons butter over moderate heat. In a heavy skillet, heat the remaining 4 tablespoons of butter with the oil. When the butter foam begins to subside, add the steaks, which have been dried on paper towels. Sauté them for 3 or 4 minutes on each side. The steaks can also be broiled. Place the steaks on the bread and arrange them on a hot plate. Set an artichoke heart filled with potatoes on each. If the hearts are small, surround them with potatoes. Serve the béarnaise sauce separately. Additional potatoes may also be served separately.

This old Parisian recipe is excellent for an informal party. The labeling of the meat is an amusing conversation topic.

Trim, wash, and slice the leek. Trim, wash, and halve the celery stalk. Peel the carrots and turnip, and cut them into large chunks. To make the stock, place the onion, the vegetables, the veal bone or chicken carcass, salt, peppercorns, and bouquet garni in a large saucepan, with the water, and bring to a boil. If possible, cook the stock in an earthenware pot with an asbestos mat underneath for protection. As soon as the water boils, skim, lower the heat, cover, and cook gently for at least 1 hour, 2 if possible. Then strain the stock, discard the vegetables and the bouquet garni, return it to the pot, and reheat to boiling.

Trim the meat. Tie each piece like a package, with a long string. Tie labels, each one with the name of a guest, on the one end of the strings. Ask each person if he wants his meat well done or rare, and label accordingly. Plunge the meat into the boiling stock. For rare beef, simmer for 25 minutes. For well done meat, cook for 30 minutes or even longer.

Remove the meat, serve with mustard, pickles, coarse salt, and baked potatoes.

Steaks in Stock

BOEUF À LA FICELLE

Serves 4

1 leek
1 celery stalk
4 small carrots
1 turnip
1 onion, peeled and stuck with
   3 cloves
1 large veal bone, chopped in half,
   or a chicken carcass
2 tsps. salt
5 peppercorns
bouquet garni
9 cups water
2 lbs. beef tenderloin, cut into
   4 thick slices

It seems that this dish was invented only a century ago, supposedly in Saint-Germain-en-Laye, at the grand opening of the railway. The cook in charge was trying to make fried potatoes. The train was late. He put them back in the oil. . . .

Peel the potatoes and slice them into rounds about ⅛ inch thick. You should have about 8 cups. Dry them well—this is important. Heat the oil in a deep skillet to very hot, 360 on a frying thermometer. (Another guide is to add a small cube of bread—it should turn golden brown within half a minute.) Add the potatoes, a few at a time, and cook over high heat until they rise to the surface and are lightly colored. Remove them from the oil and cool. Reheat the oil to 400 and fry the potatoes a second time until they are swollen and golden brown. Remove them from the oil and drain on paper towels. Place the potatoes in a hot serving dish. Season with salt and pepper and serve at once.

Soufflé Potatoes

POMMES DE TERRE
SOUFFLÉES

Serves 6

4 large potatoes
oil for deep-frying

Crêpes Suzette

CRÊPES SUZETTE

Serves 4

1 cup sifted all-purpose flour
2 eggs
½ cup water
½ cup light ale or beer

FOR THE BUTTER:
20 sugar cubes
4 small oranges or tangerines
¼ cup butter, softened
bacon fat
1 cup sifted confectioners sugar
8 tsps. Cointreau or curaçao

This desert is typical of Paris. There is, however, a legend which maintains that crêpes Suzette were created by the head chef of the Hotel de Paris *in Monte Carlo, in honor of King Edward VII of England, who was dining there with an actress named Suzette. Traditionally, tangerines are used, though the dish is also excellent when made with oranges.*

For the batter, place the sifted flour in a bowl and make a well in the center. Add the eggs, water, beer, and a pinch of salt. Mix in the center of the bowl, gradually drawing in the flour from the sides. When ingredients are blended, beat to a smooth batter. (The batter can also be prepared in an electric blender. In this case, place the eggs, water, and salt in the blender. Add the flour and then the beer. Cover and blend for a few seconds at high speed.) Let the batter stand for 30 minutes to make it lighter.

Meanwhile, prepare the orange butter. Rub the sugar cubes over the unpeeled fruit to absorb the flavor. Then crush the cubes and mix them into the slightly softened butter. Add a little of the fruit juice from the oranges or tangerines to taste.

Heat a small skillet or pancake pan and, when hot, lightly grease it with a piece of bacon fat. Pour a little of the batter into the pan. Make a pancake, toss it, then discard it, for the first one is rarely successful. Rub the pan again with the bacon fat, reheat, and pour about 2 tablespoons of batter into the pan. Tip the pan so that the batter spreads thinly over the surface. As soon as the edges turn golden brown and bubbles start to burst and form little holes on the surface, turn the pancake over. Cook for a moment. Spread each pancake with a little of the orange butter, fold it in half twice, and place it on a hot flat dish. When all the pancakes are made and filled, dredge them with confectioners sugar. Pour on the warm liqueur and ignite it with a match. Bring the flaming crêpes to the table.

It is important that the skillet or pancake pan be neither too hot nor too cool. If it is too hot, the pancake will cook too rapidly and be tough. If the pan is too cool, the immediate browning will be insufficient and the pancake will be a pale, underdone color. After each pancake has been cooked, wipe the skillet with a paper towel, regrease it lightly, and heat to the correct temperature.

Menu Planning and Wine Guide

A French meal usually consists of four or five or even six courses, all artfully blended in terms of flavors and textures, colors and patterns. The courses are balanced and well-correlated; repetition is avoided. One would never, for example, serve poached eggs as an appetizer and an omelet as entrée or dessert. Nor would a thoughtful cook prepare a meal that included creamed beans and veal in cream. A filling *quiche* would rarely be served before an elaborate entrée of *tournedos Henri IV*. Each course is considered in terms of the entire meal—there must be contrast and continuity.

Several factors will influence you in menu planning. The nature of the occasion is probably most important, followed by the season of the year. In warm weather you might prefer light, refreshing meals that can be prepared without making the kitchen excessively hot. In winter hearty soups and sophisticated desserts are appropriate. The availability of ingredients is another seasonal variable. Use fruits and vegetables that are in season and try to use local specialties as much as possible. Devote time and attention to the selection of your ingredients—the better they are the better the finished dish will be.

The sample menus which follow are only a guide. Make substitutions/additions/deletions according to season and availability of ingredients. For example, if your market has beautiful artichokes but the eggplants you had planned to buy are blemished and unappetizing in appearance, change your menu to include the artichokes.

As you plan your menu, you should give consideration to the wine. In cooking, wine heightens the character of certain dishes. It should be used only when called for as an ingredient. The alcohol is usually evaporated and only the flavor remains so you should use a high-quality wine, brandy, or liqueur.

Wine can be broadly classified into three categories: fortified wines, sparkling wines, and table wines. A fortified wine is one to which alcohol has been added, generally bringing its alcoholic content up to between 17 and 21 percent. Sherry, port, and Madeira are thus fortified. Aperitif wines, such as vermouth, are fortified and flavored with herbs. Fortified wines are served before or after a meal, rarely with it. Sparkling wines are produced throughout France and the United States, but true champagne can be made only within the district of that name, about 90 miles from

Paris. Champagne can be served as an aperitif, through the meal, or by itself as a celebration drink.

Table wines are red, rosé, or white. Strictly defined, table wines contain 14 percent or less of alcohol and are served with meals. A table wine can be a *vin ordinaire* (an inexpensive wine of anonymous origin) or a great château-bottled vintage wine.

All red table wines are dry. In making red wine, the grapes are pressed and their skins, which contain the acid tannin, remain and ferment along with the juice. The skin gives the juice its red color and also a degree of acidity. Just how much acidity depends on the amount of tannin present in the particular skin. This amount also determines just how dry the wine will be.

Rosé is made from grapes similar to those used for red wine. However, the skins are removed immediately after pressing. Basically, a rosé is an incomplete red wine and although pleasant, it rarely has the character of a good red or white wine.

White wine is produced from either red grapes that have not reached complete ripeness or green grapes. The juice generally ferments without the skins, so white wines contain less tannin than reds. This accounts for the basic taste difference between the two. White wines can run anywhere from extra dry to extremely sweet.

When serving a red wine, open it about a half hour before pouring; when you serve it, fill the glass only halfway. This gives the wine an opportunity to gather oxygen from the air, allowing it to develop the full strength of its bouquet. It is best served at room temperature (60-65°). Rosé and white wines should be chilled, but not icy. About 2 hours in the refrigerator is optimum.

There are no hard and fast rules regarding what wine to serve with what food. You should drink a wine that pleases your personal taste. For the uncertain, the following traditional pairings can be used as a guide:

Fish and shellfish: a light or medium dry white wine
Poultry and white meat: a dry white or light red wine
Hors d'oeuvre: a light, dry white or a light red wine
Red meat and game: a red wine
Cheese: red or a dry white wine
Sweet dessert: a sweet white wine

There are naturally exceptions to this guide: roast chicken for example is delicious with a red wine. Bear in mind that the richer the dish, the richer the wine should be.

When you buy wine be aware of the brand name—it identifies the shipper and the importer. The wine name tells you the geographic area in which the wine was produced. When you find a wine you like, remember the name of the district and try other wines from that area.

The menus which follow are composed almost entirely of recipes to be found in this book. Once again, they are only a guide. Wine suggestions are offered, indicating appropriate wines.

SCALLOPS IN WHITE WINE
LEG OF LAMB CASSEROLE
LETTUCE SALAD
CAMEMBERT
PLUM PIE
Muscadet

❧

RAW VEGETABLES WITH GARLIC MAYONNAISE
BRAISED BEEF
BOILED POTATOES
LETTUCE SALAD
JAM OMELET
Red Burgundy

❧

CHEESE BOATS
GAME SALAD
ROQUEFORT
FRESH FRUIT
Bordeaux

❧

BRAISED ARTICHOKES
SWEET AND SOUR HAM
STEAMED RICE
CHESTNUT PUDDING
Cider or beer

❧

GOUGÈRE
EGGS POACHED IN RED WINE
HONEY SPICE CAKE
CAMEMBERT
Red Burgundy

DUCK PÂTÉ
ONION TART
LETTUCE SALAD
BRIE
FRESH FRUIT
Beaujolais

❧

SOLE AND MUSSELS
FRESH ASPARAGUS
LETTUCE SALAD
PONT L'ÉVÊQUE
BLACK CURRANT ICE CREAM
SWEET BUTTER COOKIES
Chablis

❧

CREAMED MUSHROOMS ON TOAST
LIVER DUMPLINGS
LETTUCE SALAD
CHERRY PUDDING
White Burgundy

❧

SALAD NIÇOISE
LEMON PIE
Rosé

❧

CRAYFISH IN WHITE WINE
RABBIT WITH MUSTARD SAUCE
ARTICHOKE MOUSSE
STRAWBERRY CUSTARD PIE
Dry white wine
Red Burgundy

CONSOMMÉ
TROUT IN CHAMPAGNE
VEAL STEW
BOILED RICE
CARROT SOUFFLÉ
PLUM PIE
Champagne

❧

CHESTNUT SOUP
SHAD WITH SORREL AND BACON
BOILED POTATOES
STRAWBERRY CUSTARD PIE
Dry white wine

❧

SPINACH TARTLETS
GARNISHED STEAKS WITH BÉARNAISE SAUCE
LETTUCE SALAD
VANILLA CREAM PIE
Red Burgundy

❧

BOILED BEEF
BUTTERED NOODLES
CAMEMBERT
BLACK CURRANT ICE CREAM
SWEET BUTTER COOKIES
Burgundy

❧

ONION TART
CHICKEN IN WHITE WINE
STEAMED POTATOES
LETTUCE SALAD
LEMON PIE
Dry white wine

CREAM OF PEA SOUP
PARTRIDGE PIE
ARTICHOKE MOUSSE
CRÊPES SUZETTE
Dry white wine

❧

FRESHWATER FISH IN RED WINE
BRAISED BEEF
BOILED POTATOES
SALAD WITH ROQUEFORT DRESSING
FRESH FRUIT
Burgundy

❧

LIVER DUMPLINGS
CHICKEN WITH JUNIPER
FRIED MUSHROOMS
BLACK CURRANT ICE CREAM
SWEET BUTTER COOKIES
Bordeaux

❧

QUICHE LORRAINE
STEAK WITH WHITE WINE SAUCE
MUSHROOM SOUFFLÉ
LETTUCE SALAD
ASSORTED CHEESES
LEMON PIE
Burgundy

❧

SHRIMP COCKTAIL
ROAST PORK WITH CIDER
SAUTÉED POTATOES
FRESH FRUIT
Beaujolais

Guide to Dining Out

The major difference in dining customs between France and the United States is the number of courses traditionally ordered by Frenchmen. The main meal of the day may consist of four to eight courses, served one after the other.

A common practice of many French restaurants is to display a menu in the window. It will probably show the price of à la carte dishes, complete meals (*prix fixe*) and the daily special (*plat du jour*). The menu will usually advise if there is a cover charge (*couvert*) or a service charge (*service 10%*), and if wine or beer is included in the price of the meal (known as *boissons comprises*). A service charge is that percentage of your bill that is automatically added as a tip by the restaurant. You may add to this amount if you choose. Where there is no service charge, you normally tip about 15% of your total bill.

Excellent food is served in a variety of French restaurants. If you choose to eat in a popular French restaurant, it is wise to phone for a reservation in advance. Lunch (*le déjeuner*) is generally served from noon to 3 P.M. Dinner (*le dîner*) is eaten around 8 P.M. Expect solicitous and leisurely service. In the fine restaurants, most dishes are prepared to order. Though you may have to wait a bit, you won't be served overcooked beans or warmed-up mushrooms.

If you are going to have wine with your meal, ask to see the wine list right after you've made your menu selection. The wine should be coordinated with the food. In a fine restaurant the wine steward (*sommelier*) will take care of your wine needs. White wine should be chilled, but not overly so. This could occur if the white wine is served at the beginning of your meal and stays in a bucket of ice until your main course is served. To avoid overchilling merely take the wine out of the bucket and let it stand on the table.

When he brings the wine to your table he shows you the bottle. You should check to be sure it's the wine you ordered and of the vintage stated on the wine list. After the bottle is opened, make sure the cork is in one piece (if not, pieces of cork may be in the wine) and does not smell sour. And remember, when you taste the wine your purpose is to find out if the wine is good, to know if it has turned sour, or contains sediment. These are the only reasons you should ever return a wine. Whether or not you like the wine, assuming it tastes as it should, is not a legitimate reason to ask the *sommelier* for a replacement.

Dining out need not be confined to a restaurant. The French countryside is an open invitation to picnicing and few could think of a better way to spend a lazy summer afternoon. Many hotels and restaurants will supply an excellent picnic basket of local pâtes and sausage, bread still warm from the oven, a good selection of cheese and fruit, or a sweet, and naturally, a bottle of the local vineyard's best.

In France, as in America, you will find many types of eating and drinking places. Here are the most common.

French Name	Description
Auberge	An inn, usually found in the country, that serves full meals.
Bistro	Comparable to an English pub. A simple restaurant where drinks and snacks are served, often very good, and where one does not have to dress.
Boîte (de nuit)	A nightclub.
Brasserie	A café where food and drink are served at all times.
Café	A coffeehouse. Snacks are offered, but seldom meals.
Relais	A country inn; menus of all sorts—from snacks to grand dinners.
Restaurant	Restaurants are classified by the standard of the cuisine and service.
Restoroute	A large highway restaurant; waiter service and/or self-service.
Routier	Comparable to our diner.
Snack-Bar	Snackbar.

French menus often contain large numbers of food categories: soups, appetizers, entrées, vegetables, salads, cheeses, desserts, fruit, and nonalcoholic beverages. The menus on the following pages contain some of the more popular and traditional dishes you are apt to find in small classic restaurants as well as restaurants of a grander sort.

Grande Cuisine

POTAGES (soups)

POTAGE GERMINY
sorrel soup

MARMITE DIEPPOISE
fish soup with a creamy base

HORS D'OEUVRE (appetizers)

TRUFFES SOUS LA CENDRE
whole truffles cooked in ashes

FOIE GRAS EN BRIOCHE
goose liver in a brioche

OMELETTE AUX TRUFFES
omelet with truffles

JAMBON À LA BOURGUIGNONNE
ham in parslied jelly

AVOCAT AU CRABE
avocado stuffed with crabmeat

ASPERGES SAUCE MOUSSELINE
asparagus in a butter and cream sauce

POISSONS (fish)

TRUITE AU BLEU
scalded trout

SOLE BONNE FEMME
Dover sole with mushrooms

TURBOT SAUCE HOLLANDAISE
turbot with hollandaise sauce

HOMARD GRILLÉ
broiled lobster

BAR FLAMBÉ
flamed bass

ENTRÉES (main courses)

CANARD MONTMORENCY
duck with cherries

GIGOT EN CROÛTE
leg of lamb in a pastry case

CÔTE DE BOEUF À LA MOELLE
rib steak, with poached marrow

ESCALOPES ARCHIDUC
*veal scallops in a cream,
Madeira, and cheese sauce*

TOURNEDOS ROSSINI
*filet mignon with goose liver
and artichoke bottom*

GRIVES AU GENIÈVRE
thrushes with juniper sauce

CAILLES AUX RAISINS
quail with grapes

DINDE AU PORTO
turkey in port wine sauce

LÉGUMES (vegetables)

HARICOTS VERTS
string beans

POMMES SOUFFLÉES
*thin slices of potatoes
puffed in two oil baths*

GRATIN DAUPHINOIS
sliced potatoes with cream

CÈPES FARCIS
stuffed mushrooms

POMMES ANNA
baked sliced potatoes

PURÉE DE MARRONS
chestnut puree

SALADES (salads)

SALADE DE CRESSON
watercress

LAITUE AU CITRON
lettuce with lemon dressing

SALADE D'HIVER
endives, nuts, apples, etc.

FROMAGES (cheeses)

ROQUEFORT, MUNSTER, BANON, BRIE, REBLOCHON, GRUYÈRE, COULOMMIERS, PICODON

DESSERTS (desserts)

SORBET AU CASSIS
black currant sherbert

DIPLOMATE GLACÉ
ladyfingers and ice cream cake

GATEAU FORÊT NOIRE
chocolate and cherries cake

PROFITEROLLES
cream puffs

GLACE AUX MARRONS
chestnut ice cream

POIRES BOURDALOUE
pear and custard open tart

Cuisine Bourgeoise

POTAGES (*soups*)

POTAGE DU BARRY
cauliflower soup

VELOUTÉ AUX CHAMPIGNONS
mushroom cream soup

SOUPE À L'OIGNON
onion soup

SOUPE DE POISSONS
fish soup

HORS D'OEUVRE (*appetizers*)

PÂTÉ DE CANARD
pâté of duck

TOMATES À L'ANTIBOISE
*raw tomatoes filled with tuna
fish and mayonnaise*

CÉLERI RÉMOULADE
chopped celeriac with mustardy sauce

MOULES MARINIÈRE
*mussels cooked in white wine,
served on half shell*

SAUCISSON D'ARLES
sliced dry sausage

OEUFS EN MEURETTE
eggs cooked in red wine sauce

ENTRÉES (*main courses*)

BOUILLABAISSE
fish stew

GIGOT BRETONNE
leg of lamb with white beans

TRIPES À LA MODE DE CAEN
tripe with wine and applejack

BOEUF SAUCE MADÈRE
roast beef with Madeira sauce

SOLE DIEPPOISE
*Dover sole with mussels, shrimps,
mushrooms, and cream sauce*

LAPIN DE GARENNE AUX PRUNEAUX
wild rabbit with prunes

CÔTES DE VEAU GRAND-MÈRE
*veal chops with small onions,
mushrooms, and potatoes*

COQ AU VIN
chicken in white wine sauce

LÉGUMES (*vegetables*)

PETITS POIS À LA BOURGEOISE
*peas with lettuce, onions,
and bacon*

POMMES SAUTÉES
stir-fried potatoes

NAVETS AU VERMOUTH
turnips in vermouth sauce

POMMES MOUSSELINE
light mashed potatoes

ÉPINARDS À LA CRÈME
creamed spinach

POMMES PAILLE
straw potatoes

RATATOUILLE
*eggplant, zucchini, tomato,
green pepper stew*

ENDIVES BRAISÉES
endives cooked in Dutch oven

POMMES FRITES
French-fried potatoes

RIZ À LA TOMATE
rice with tomato sauce

SALADES (*salads*)

SALADE NICQISE
tomato, tuna, anchovy fillets

PISSENLITS AU LARD
dandelion with melted bacon

LAITUE MIMOSA
lettuce with hard-boiled eggs

SALADE DE CRESSON
watercress

FROMAGES (*cheeses*)

CAMEMBERT, CANTAL, PORT-SALUT, CHABICHOU, COEUR À LA CRÈME, COMTÉ

DESSERTS (*desserts*)

MOUSSE AU CHOCOLAT
chocolate mousse

SORBET AU CITRON
lemon sherbert

CRÈME RENVERSÉE
baked custard

CLAFOUTIS
cherry cake, moist and custardy

Index

Those entries which appear in SMALL CAPITAL LETTERS are the French recipe titles.

Illustrations and Photographs

cross the flooded river ?

For Bonzo

KINGFISHER
Larousse Kingfisher Chambers Inc.
95 Madison Avenue
New York, New York 10016

First American edition, 1995

2 4 6 8 10 9 7 5 3 1

Cataloging-in-Publication Data has been applied for

ISBN 1-85697-564-9

Printed in Italy

OUT TO LUNCH

PRISCILLA LAMONT

Kingfisher

NEW YORK

Mr. Howgego and Mrs. Burdle
were the best of friends.

But on one matter they were altogether different.
Mr. Howgego was never late for anything,
and Mrs. Burdle was never on time.

"Better late than never," Mrs. Burdle would say.
"Better never late," would come the reply.
"On the dot, like clockwork, that's me."

Mrs. Burdle was fed up with being told off.
"I'll show him how 'on the dot' I can be,"
she thought and for a whole week she
practiced being everywhere on time.

Finally she invited Mr. Howgego for
lunch, at twelve o'clock sharp.
"Everything will be
ready *on the dot*,"
she said firmly.

On the dot of seven, Mrs. Burdle woke up
when her alarm clock rang.
"Just like clockwork!" she smiled.

But Mr. Howgego did not wake up.
He had overwound his clock and
it had stopped working altogether.

On the dot of eight, Mrs. Burdle was busy
making the pastry for a scrumptious
chicken and ham pie.

8 o'clock
measure out
ingredients
for pie
8.30 o'clock
chop up all
p.t.o

And Mr. Howgego woke up with a bump —
A WHOLE HOUR LATE!
"Dear me," he said to himself. "No time to lose."

On the dot of nine, Mrs. Burdle put her pie in the oven and went to pick some watercress for the soup.

Mr. Howgego, however, was in a bit of a muddle.
"Now, now," he told himself severely.
"More haste, less speed!"

On the dot of ten, the watercress soup
was bubbling away and the pie was
beautifully cooked. Mrs. Burdle hummed a
tune as she mixed the dessert ingredients.

Mr. Howgego, after some delay,
managed to start up his automobile.
"Of course!" he cried. "The short cut will
save me time." And he sped on his way.

On the dot of eleven, the sun was shining, and Mrs. Burdle set the table by the apple tree. After that she went indoors to wash her paws and whiskers before lunch.

Meanwhile, Mr. Howgego
found the road flooded.
He missed his way
and drove straight
into the river.
Just in time
he managed to
grab a branch
as the automobile
sank
beneath
him...

On the dot of twelve,
Mrs. Burdle was quite ready
to welcome her guest.

He, on the other hand,
was sitting mournfully on his branch
as it drifted gently out to sea.

On the dot of one, Mrs. Burdle
was really hungry.
"Like clockwork?" she complained.
"Fiddlesticks!"

At the same time, a bedraggled Mr. Howgego
was being rescued by a passing fishing boat.
"Well, late I may be, but at least I'm safe,"
he muttered as he nibbled
on a ship's biscuit.

On the dot of two, Mrs. Burdle said,
"Drat Mr. Howgego! I shan't let it
all go to waste."
Impatiently, she took a large mouthful.

By this time, Mr. Howgego was safely ashore
again. And although he was dreadfully late,
it hardly seemed to matter anymore.

On the dot of three, Mrs. Burdle was feeling very sleepy in the pleasant afternoon sunshine.

And Mr. Howgego suddenly found
himself getting quite carried away!

There he was,
floating high
above the ground.
"How exhilarating!"
he exclaimed.

He looked down,
and to his
surprise, he saw
a familiar roof,
far below.

As the balloon
gradually descended,
he recognized
dear Mrs. Burdle.
Mr. Howgego leaned out
to get a better look and...

On the dot of four, Mr. Howgego finally
arrived, right on top of the dessert.
"Oh! There you are at last," exclaimed
Mrs. Burdle. "And only *four* hours late."

"Er, yes," replied Mr. Howgego,
blushing slightly. "But as *you*
always say, Mrs. Burdle,
better late than never!"

Can you help Mr. Howgego